Enjoy!

An Incomplete but
Highly Esteemed List . . .

140-Character Fairy Tale Characters

Strange Mysteries

*He Liked to
Hip Hop All Around*

*Cinderella's Bad Day,
Prince Charming is a Monster,
and Other Tragic Love Tales*

Don't Stay Up So Late

*If I Ever Saw
Mr. JK I Would Ask Him These
Things*

*A Visitors Guide: See Ann Arbor by
Train, Plane, or Automobile*

*Somebody Said You Were
Looking for Me*

*Thunder-, Lightning-, &
Waterproof!*

...of Other Books Published by 826michigan

When the Whales Celebrate

826michigan OMNIBUS, Vol. 4

All I Could Do Was Look Up: Anatomy of a Middle School

Dr. Von Humor's Encyclopedia of Monster Botany

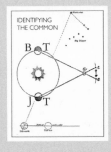

Identifying the Common Bot Jot

Maybe You Can Cook Me Up Some Oatmeal Before You Save the World

826michigan OMNIBUS, 5th Edition

What to Call the Place I Call Home

The Distance Between Two Sides of a Color

Enjoy!

Recipes for Building Community

826michigan staff

Amanda Uhle · Executive Director
Amy Sumerton · Program Director
Catherine Calabro · Education Director
Amy Wilson · Communications Coordinator
Frances Martin · Program Manager & Volunteer Coordinator
D'Real Graham · Program Coordinator
Courtney Randolph · Program Manager & Volunteer Coordinator
Brandan Pierce · Program Assistant

Copyright © 2014 by 826michigan and Blotch Books.

All rights reserved by 826michigan, the many whims of
Dr. Thaddeus Blotch, and the authors.

No part of this book may be reproduced without express written
permission from the publisher, except for small excerpts for the
purposes of review or scholarly study.

ISBN 978-0-9827293-6-6

By purchasing this book, other publications from 826michigan,
and robot wares, you are helping 826michigan continue to offer
free student programs.

For more information, please visit:
www.826michigan.org

826michigan
115 East Liberty Street • Ann Arbor, MI 48104
734.761.3463 • 826michigan.org

Printed in Dexter, Michigan by Thomson-Shore.

Book Design: Kevin Woodland
Design Assistant: Jill Epstein

Copyeditors: Nicole Brugger-Dethmers, Jessi Carrothers, Jill
Epstein, Megan Gilson, Kimberly Huebner, Rachael Jackson,
Erica Jolokai, Jennifer Pulling, Rachel Rickard, Alex Schillinger,
Kati Shanks, Roger Valade

First printing
Manufactured by Thomson-Shore, Dexter, MI (USA); RMA595MS449, May, 2014

Contents

Foreword

By Ari Weinzweig

THERE ARE MANY WAYS to take stock of the current status of the American Union—millions of unique windows into what the outside world often perceives to be a singular state. The book you're holding in your hands right now is one of them. I doubt that world leaders in Washington, London, Paris, or Lagos will read it. But maybe they should.

Imagine for an instant, or maybe for the hour or so that it will take you to read this book, that a high school in Ypsilanti, Michigan, not the government in Washington or the high society of New York City, was the center of the American universe. That the views that swayed the hearts and minds that mattered were swayed, not by *The New York Times*, NPR, or CNN, but by the stories of these students. That these teenagers who were so generous in sharing their memories and family meals with us—not Wall Street brokers or Washington politicians—can best convey the core of the national soul.

Much of this book is based on food and cooking, but I would argue it's so much more than that. Each entry is as much about the accompanying narratives as about the recipes to which they're attached. The students' stories connect us to their pasts, to places in their memories, or to places they've barely, if ever, visited but of which they've heard countless tales told by their parents, grandparents, aunts, uncles, and friends.

In that sense, each story in this book calls up a scene, a family, a history, a kitchen, a connection with a mother or a grandmother, a father or a friend.

In *A Field Guide to Getting Lost,* Rebecca Solnit writes that, "The places in which any significant event occurred become embedded with some of that emotion, and to recover the memory of the place is to recover the emotion, and sometimes to revisit the place uncovers the emotion. Every love has its landscape." In that sense, each story in this book calls up a scene, a family, a history, a kitchen, a connection with a mother or a grandmother, a father or a friend. Many are about another place and in another time, both of which have been left physically behind, but of which the feelings, food, and family memories are as alive as ever.

Many are about another place and in another time, both of which have been left physically behind, but of which the feelings, food, and family memories are as alive as ever.

The stories that follow call up emotional connections for me as well—they remind me so much of the stories my grandparents used to tell me. They too came to the US as kids from another country. Food was, then as now, a way to connect their kids and grandkids with their past. For me, it was potato latkes, chopped liver, chicken soup, and roast chicken, all with roots in Russia but served up on the South Side of Chicago. For today's students, it's stuffed grape leaves, *tajadas*, hummus, *yaroa*, and *arroz guisado*

con pollo. In case cooking isn't your thing, you can also read about how to wrap an Indian sari, be in a rock band, change a tire in the middle of the road, and, of course, how to be successful in life.

All in all, this book is a pretty complete little slice of cross-cultural history here in a mid-sized city in Southeastern Michigan in the second decade of the twenty-first century. The landscape it lays out is as much internal as it is for setting out on the table. As you'll see, it's a world where memories of Michoacán are embedded in education in Michigan. Where New Delhi, Beirut, and Mexico City are the bases for memories, meals, and learnings. Savor each story and the feelings—both your own and those of the student-writers—that come with it. As Rebecca Solnit says, "The places inside matter as much as the ones outside." The contributors to this work may not—yet—be world famous writers, but their sensitivity and their sense of themselves, their past, and their place in the world bodes well for the rest of us.

RECIPES FROM OUR FRIENDS

Introduction

By Lauren Koski and Brandan Pierce

R EMEMBER THAT FEELING OF RELIEF you got in high school when you would step into your favorite classroom? Surrounded by a jungle of harassment, gossip, and tediousness, you had that one oasis in the building that offered you a reprieve from worrying about getting called on by the teacher, or your outfit, or all of the homework that awaited you that evening. You felt safe to be yourself. This is what Liz Sirman, English Language Learner (ELL) teacher at Ypsilanti Community High School, has created in her classroom. Here you will find a communal sea of snacks that rarely dries up, alongside your classmates erupting with laughter and exclamations in multiple languages: Liz is a deeply caring teacher who wants her students to succeed, whether she is texting to remind them of homework assignments or coaching them through the process of writing a resume. Those students respond in turn with respect, admiration, and a willingness to put in the effort, all while being more open with one another than you'd ever expect in a high school classroom.

Along with that openness comes an ingenuous honesty with anyone in the room. "Hey man! Why you late?" Carlos would ask, to keep volunteers accountable (regardless of polar vortex conditions, we might add). We discovered very quickly that if an assignment was confusing or didn't resonate with them, they'd voice their advice on how to make it interesting. Before the school year began, we planned to create a book in which these students could share their expertise around building community with the members of the newly consolidated Ypsilanti Community Schools district. Based on their love of sharing snacks and recipes from their home cultures, we created a series of lessons focused on food as a basis for creating and maintaining relationships. However, they challenged us to push beyond this.

Instead of just memoirs about family meals, they opened up about their first moments in America. The recipe assignment also left room to transform into "How-To" guidelines on other topics where the students could share their expertise. We learned that if we wanted students to write about their experiences building community, then we needed to open the floor to their ideas. They had already made the transition to an entirely new country, and they understood what helped them do it. They simply asked us to trust them and help them to make their writing the best it could be.

Alongside the personal narrative writing in class, an opportunity opened up that allowed Liz's students a chance to correspond with a younger audience.

With ELL teacher Shannon Fitzgerald's help, a group of multilingual students at Adams STEM Academy in Ypsilanti became pen-pals with the high school students. To say that this was cute would be a vast understatement. Picture a level of cute on par with a big-eyed kitten and puppy rolling around together, until they fall asleep in each other's grasps on top of your grandmother's lap. When the YCHS students received the letters, it was as if they had received the most precious text message of their lives. Brags of "Mine speaks Spanish!" and "Mine speaks Mandingo!" echoed through the room as students frantically opened their letters and shared them with each other. Meanwhile, at Adams, students accosted Ms. Fitzgerald in the hallway, begging for an update on their correspondence.

With the book starting to take shape, Ari Weinzweig, co-founder and co-owner of Zingerman's Community of Businesses, invited Liz Sirman's class to the Zingerman's Deli where we tasted foods and talked about his process for writing about food. He presented the students with a classic sour cream coffee cake and talked to them about the carefully sourced international ingredients. He asked them to describe the coffee cake, to use all five senses to really experience all aspects of that slice. This finite example of descriptive writing encouraged students to expand their stories in the weeks following the field trip. The details they explored in their writing were as crucial to their storytelling as the ingredients that made up the coffee cake. These students challenged us, every day, to evaluate our own understanding of food, family, and what it means to be a person between worlds.

Whether detailing the in-and-outs of *La Posada* or describing the frigid waters of the Furat River, these students have shown their successful integration of their inherited cultures and life in Ypsilanti, Michigan.

These students challenged us, every day, to evaluate our own understanding of food, family, and what it means to be a person between worlds.

All of the beautiful, painful, hilarious, and profound thoughts that these students have written truly make this book worthy of sharing with young people and adults all over the world.

So here . . . take a look through this collection of moments that have so much to teach us about connection, and enjoy!

GUIDE

AUTHOR
BIO

PEN-PAL
LETTERS

HOW-TO

MEMOIR

OPEN
LETTER

RECIPE

Rosibel Brown

 Rosibel Brown is a sophomore at YCHS. She was born in San Juan, Puerto Rico, on July 23, 1998. She loves to travel because she likes to explore new places and meet new people. Rosibel also enjoys sports, especially basketball, softball, and baseball. She is a utility player for the Braves. Ten years from now, Rosibel sees herself becoming a doctor and taking care of people in Puerto Rico.

AGE 15

Recipe for
Arroz Guisado con Pollo

Arroz con Pollo is a typical dish in Puerto Rico. A lot of people know how to make rice with chicken, but not the way a Puerto Rican can do it. *Arroz con Pollo* is like the door of heaven. When you put it in your mouth and feel the taste, it's like you've moved to another country and are tasting the best food in the world.

This recipe is really important to me because it's my mom's favorite dish, and it's part of my family. My mom is the most important woman in my whole life. If my mom doesn't like something, I don't like it either. *Arroz con Pollo* represents my country, my culture, and my people. I'm proud of where I come from . . . I'm from Puerto Rico.

Estimated time: Twenty or thirty minutes

INGREDIENTS

- *5 tazas de arroz* (cups of cooked rice)
- *1 o 2 paquetes de pollo* (packets of chicken)
- *Adobo*
- *Sazón* (seasoning)
- *Sofrito* (lightly fried onion, garlic, peppers, cilantro, and tomato)
- *Jamón* (ham)
- *Aceite de aceituna* (olive oil)
- Salsa Goya

DIRECTIONS

1. *Poner una olla con aceite a fuego lento.* (Put a pan with oil on low heat.)

2. *Agregue el sofrito junto con el jamón y dejarlo un rato friendóse.* (Add the vegetables together with the ham and leave it a moment to fry.)

3. *Luego agregue la Salsa Goya, después lo mueve para que todo se mezcla junto con el sazón.* (Later, add the Goya Salsa or sauce, then move it around so that it mixes in together with the seasoning.)

4. *Agregas agua y la cantidad de pollo que le quiera echar.* (Add water and the amount of chicken that you want to put in.)

5. *Deja el pollo por un rato para que se cocine junto con los otros ingredientes.* (Leave the chicken for a moment so that it can cook together with the other ingredients.)

6. *Luego agregas el arroz y lo dejas como por veinte o treinta minutos.* (Later add the rice and let it sit for twenty or thirty minutes.)

My Childhood in Puerto Rico

I WAS BORN JULY 23, 1998, in San Juan, Puerto Rico. San Juan is the most important city in Puerto Rico because it is the capital. San Juan is beautiful, and when I say beautiful, I really mean beautiful. In San Juan there is this big building called *El Morro*. *El Morro* is a big wall that people used to protect themselves back in the days when there was a war.

Puerto Rico is a gorgeous country. There are beautiful beaches. It's way different than here because it is always hot and you feel more free. I feel so happy when I'm in Puerto Rico because it is my country and because everybody speaks the same language. I'm in love with my country. In Puerto Rico, we are always having parties.

I grew up in a very small town called Loiza. My family and I all lived in this same town. My early childhood was awesome. I remember being outside playing with my cousin and arguing over a Barbie. It was funny. My first day in preschool was the best day in my life. I was smarter than everybody.

My family and I moved to the USA in 2010; I was eleven years old. My family and I have only been here for three years, but it feels like ten years. My birthday is the most important event in my life and my family's life because I am the little one.

I miss Puerto Rico so much. It's hard for me to get used to this weather. Winter is really long. When I was in Puerto Rico, it was always hot. It was really hard for me and my family to get used to new weather, a new country, and a new language.

My plan for my future is to finish high school, go to college, become a doctor, and never fall in love again. Single for life!

Homecoming Dance

I WENT TO THE PEP RALLY and the game. It was a long day. I got home at 11:00PM, and I was so tired. And then I had to wake up around six in the morning to get my dress. I had to wait for close to three hours because my mom and my sister Rochely were taking forever. I was hungry, so I made something for my little niece Yeichalys and myself.

Before I could leave for the dance, I had to do a lot of things, like clean my room, clean the bathroom, and cook. My mom told me that if I didn't do those things, I was not going to be able to go to the dance. One of my friends came over to my house because she didn't have a ride. I felt bad because she had to wait for me for like an hour. But finally we were able to leave for the dance.

I got to the dance and looked around. The cafeteria was looking nice. The school had decorated. It was like a disco. They put all the tables in the back, and they closed the stairs. The first person I saw dancing was my best friend. I was so happy when I saw him. Everybody was looking nice . . . well, not *everybody*, but most of them. I started dancing with my friends. Somebody who I didn't even know asked me to dance, and I said yes. Everybody was close to each other, and somebody found a tampon on the floor. I was about to throw up! But I had fun. Everybody was talking about my dress, because it was so cute, and my shoes, too! My dress was black and short, and my back showed a little. I had on really tall black shoes. I was looking like a woman.

After the dance, we went out to eat. We went to Applebee's, and we ate a lot of meat with BBQ. We ate a lot of ice cream. We saw other people there from our school, and we were laughing together and making fun of the other people who we saw there.

This was a memorable event to me because it was the Homecoming Dance. Everyone in the school was waiting for it for a long time. It's the most important dance, and I went because I wanted to support my school.

Open Letter

Dear Ypsilanti Community High School,

In order to make our school greater, we should make some changes to make our school feel safe and fun. Instead of having two lunches, we should have three lunches, because the second lunch has too many people and some of the students don't even get to eat.

I would like for people to work in groups more. That's a good way for students to get to know one another. We should support one another more, like in our basketball games, football games, volleyball games, and more.

Teachers should communicate more with one another to make our school better. Some of the teachers don't communicate with the students. That's why some of the students have problems in their classes or in school. For example, some of the teachers don't know how to explain very well what they want us to do. They could also make our classes more fun for us.

I went to a game on Tuesday, and they had a lot more security than during school hours. I think that we should have more security during school hours than at games.

Also, I think that the buses should be dismissed in a more organized way and have more security.

I am a student from Ypsilanti Community High School who wants to make this school better; I want people to respect my school. I also have the experience of coming from another country and have had to learn how to make a new community. In my third-hour class, we are all from different countries and we get along as a family. My hope is that one day our school will get along as a family, like my third hour.

Sincerely,

Rosibel Brown

Amber Vongphachanh

 Amber Vongphachanh was born in Ypsilanti, Michigan. She speaks Laotian and English. Her favorite food is pizza. Amber likes to go outside and play with her brothers and sisters. When she grows up, she wants to be a doctor. She likes to go out with her family to dinner. Her favorite books are *Junie B. Jones* and *Judy Moody*.

AGE 11

Recipe for Peanut Butter and Jelly

INGREDIENTS

- Bread
- Peanut butter
- Jelly

DIRECTIONS

1. Get your bread.
2. Get your plate.
3. Get jelly.
4. Get peanut butter.
5. Then, put jelly on your bread, and peanut butter.
6. Put another slice of bread on top, or fold the bread if you need to.

Pen-pal Letters

Dear pen-pal,

My name is Amber, and I am in fifth grade. I am eleven years old. My favorite subject is math. My favorite sports are soccer and basketball. What are your favorite sports and subjects? I have three brothers and one sister. I love to play with my sister the most. How many sisters or brothers do you have? My favorite books are *Junie B. Jones* and *Judy Moody*. I was born in 2002, on June 18. My full name is Amber Vongphachanh. I know that I have lots of letters in my last name. Lots of people ask me, "Why do you have lots of letters in your last name?" My favorite colors are green and pink. I want to be a doctor when I grow up. My favorite candies are Jolly Ranchers.

Sincerely,

Amber

Dear Amber,

My name is Rosibel. I am fifteen years old, and I'm in tenth grade. My favorite subjects are chemistry and gym. My favorite sports are basketball, softball, and baseball. I have two sisters and one brother. I'm the young one. I was born on July 23, 1998. Yeah, I'm kind of old. My full name is Rosibel Brown Pizarro. A lot of people call me Pizza because my last name sounds like you are saying pizza. My favorite colors are pink, red, and yellow. My favorite artist is Nicki Minaj. I want to be a doctor, too! I love helping people feel better. My favorite candy is Jolly Ranchers, too! We both like a lot of the same things. I love the color of your letter. It is so beautiful, and the flowers are so colorful—I love them. I will love to meet you one day and eat a lot of Jolly Ranchers together.

Sincerely,

Rosibel

....

Dear Rosibel,

How are you? YOUR letter was enjoyable. I am Asian. I am from Laos. My favorite places to go are California and Las Vegas. My favorite song is "The Way" by Ariana Grande. My favorite holidays are Christmas and Easter Day. My favorite shoes are Jordans. I really like your handwriting. Well, that's enough writing for me. Bye! Can't wait for your next letter. Oh! I forgot to tell you about a holiday tradition. For Christmas, I play with my cousins with my Christmas things. I have a Christmas tree. What do you do for your tradition? What's your favorite movie? Do you have a dog?

Sincerely,

Amber

Dear Amber,

I'm doing great. I'm so happy that you liked my letter. I am Puerto Rican from Puerto Rico, which means I'm Hispanic. My favorite places to go are New York, Puerto Rico, Los Angeles, and Las Vegas. My favorite songs are "I Love the Way" by Ariana Grande, "High School" by Nicki Minaj, and "Love More" by Chris Brown and Nicki Minaj. My favorite holidays are Christmas and Thanksgiving, because you are being thankful for the things that God has given you. My favorite shoes are Jordans, Levis, and Adidas. I'm so happy that you like my handwriting; I think it is ugly, but it doesn't really matter. For my tradition for Christmas, I spend time with family and I eat a lot because I love food! I mean, who doesn't love food? And I have a beautiful Christmas tree. My favorite movies are *Home Alone* and *The Grinch*. I don't have a dog but I would love to have one. My parents won't let me. I can't wait for your next letter!

Sincerely,

Rosibel <3

....

Dear Rosibel,

I am glad to write to you again, Rosibel. What kind of things do you do over break? I do things like watch TV and get on the iPad and iPhone. Do you go outside and play with snow? I don't, because the snow is too cold and my hand hurts. Have you made a snowman or snowgirl? I haven't, because I don't know how to make it. I always tried. Oh yeah, my favorite boy singer is Chris Brown, too; I just forgot. And my favorite food experience is Thanksgiving because the turkey is so delicious! What's your favorite food experience, Rosibel?

Sincerely,

Amber

Dear Amber,

I'm so happy that you wrote back. I was so happy when I saw your letter. I didn't really do anything on break. I did the same things that you did. I love going outside to play with the snow, and I made a snowman over break. My favorite food experience is turkey, too. I love turkey.

Sincerely,

Rosibel

....

Dear Rosibel,

How are you? I am happy I am writing back to you again. How is your school like a family? My school's name is Adams. The school is fun. It's filled with nice teachers and it's filled up with nice other kids. My school is like a family because we all get along, we feel great in the same class. We see each other every five days. We eat together at lunch. We go on a field trip like a family.

Sincerely,

Amber Vongphachanh

Dear Amber,

I'm really good and happy to write you again. My school is like a family to me, especially my second and third hour, because there are a lot of people from different countries, and we are always sharing food and making parties. My school's name is Ypsilanti Community High School—long name, right?? LOL.

Sincerely,

Rosibel Brown

....

Dear Rosibel,

I am really happy writing you back again, Rosibel. Over break, I stayed home and watched TV and did other things. But over break I was sick, it was really bad. And yeah, that's a long name for your school. At my school, it's a short name. It's called Adams Academy.

HI!!!

xoxo

Amber

EVE ARONOFF

PRESENTS

SEARED SCALLOPS WITH MAPLE CREAM AND OHIO BACON

Eve Aronoff is the chef and owner of Frita Batidos and author of *eve: Contemporary Cuisine, Méthode Traditionnelle*. A graduate of Le Cordon Bleu in Paris, France, Eve's previous restaurant, eve, rose to national recognition and received praise from Chefs Mario Batali and Alice Waters.

This is a recipe I came up with just after our cookbook was published, so it is not included in the book, but it is special because it is a personal favorite. It reminds me of days cooking at eve, and I also love it because it is such a simple recipe but with so much flavor! It also highlights one of my favorite and most delicious ingredients ever—Nantucket Bay Scallops!

Serves four as an appetizer (multiply as desired as an entrée)

INGREDIENTS

- 8 large fresh sea scallops (or ¾ of a pound Nantucket Bay Scallops, in season from November through beginning of January)
- ½ pound of Ohio thick-cut bacon, cut into a fine dice
- Olive oil
- Kosher salt
- Freshly ground black pepper
- ½ cup heavy whipping cream
- 4 tablespoons maple syrup
- 2 tablespoons chives, thinly sliced

DIRECTIONS

1. Stir together cream and maple syrup, and set aside.

2. Season scallops evenly with salt and pepper.

3. Over medium heat, sauté bacon until just cooked (just pink), remove from pan, and set aside to finish dish, leaving bacon grease in pan.

4. Add some olive oil, raise heat to high, and sear scallops about two to three minutes per side.

5. If you have a broiler, spoon maple cream over scallops, sprinkle with bacon, and place under broiler to finish for about two minutes until golden and bubbly. Remove from broiler and sprinkle with chives to finish. If you do not have a broiler, warm maple cream slightly and spoon over scallops, and then sprinkle with bacon and chives to finish.

Wendy Caishpal-Vega

 Wendy Caishpal-Vega was born in El Salvador on December 6, 1996. She enjoys soccer and most enjoys being a goalie. She enjoys dancing and being kind. She studies at Ypsilanti Community High School. When she finishes school, she wants to become a licensed nurse.

AGE 17

Recipe for *Espaguetis con Queso*

This is a special recipe to me because I have created it on my own. It contains a special cheese from El Salvador. Everyone who has ever tried it has loved it.

INGREDIENTES

- *Espaguetis* (spaghetti)
- *Salsa de tomate, no dulce* (tomato salsa, not sweet)
- *Queso* (cheese)
- *Cebolla* (onion)
- *Tomate* (tomato)
- *Sal* (salt)
- *Aceite* (oil)
- *Consome* (flavor/bouillon cube)

DIRECTIONS

1. *Abre el paquete.* (Open the spaghetti package.)

2. *Pone en el olla con agua suficiente—no queman.* (Put enough water in a pot so it does not burn the pasta.)

3. *Hierve el agua con el espaguetis.* (Boil the water with the spaghetti.)

4. *Espera para hervir.* (Wait for the water to boil.)

5. *Espera para el espaguetis blando.* (Wait for the spaghetti to turn soft.)

6. *Saca el espaguetis. Llavar el espaguetis con agua tibia.* (Remove the spaghetti. Rinse the spaghetti with cool water.)

7. *Pone el espaguetis en el plato.* (Put the spaghetti on a plate.)

8. *Mezcla el queso con tomate y cebolla con sus manos.* (Mix the cheese with tomato and onion with your hands.)

9. *Pone el queso adentro del espaguetis.* (Put the cheese on top of the spaghetti.)

10. *Pone el sartén en la cucina con aceite.* (Put the pan on the stove with oil in the pan.)

11. *Espera para el aceite hervir.* (Wait for the oil to boil.)

12. *Pone el espaguetis en el sartén.* (Put the spaghetti in the pan.)

13. *Pone la salsa adentro del espaguetis.* (Put the salsa on top of the spaghetti.)

14. *Espera para la salsa tomar los sabores/mezclar con el espaguetis.* (Wait for the flavors from the salsa to mix with the spaghetti.)

15. *¡Listo!* (Ready!)

My Adventure

WHEN I WAS SEVEN YEARS OLD, my mother left El Salvador for the United States. She ended up working in Ypsilanti, Michigan, for ten years. Age seven was the last time I saw my mom for ten years. I lived with my dad and my little sister, who is four years younger than I am.

In January, I decided to come to the United States to be with my mom. I want to study and learn English so I can receive a strong education. I want to be a nurse, and plan to support my mother, who has worked hard for so many years.

I am now studying at Ypsilanti Community High School. When I arrived and saw all the snow and felt the frigid cold, it was completely new and strange to me. In addition, everyone was speaking English, and I could only understand Spanish. I had heard English songs before but had never been surrounded by it for an entire day! My head was killing me when I arrived home after my first day. Every day, I am learning to adjust and understand more, little by little. It keeps getting easier.

When I go home at the end of each day, I am incredibly happy to see and spend time with my mom. After being apart for ten years, it is a relief to finally be with her again. We enjoy spending time getting to know each other again.

MARIO BATALI

PRESENTS

TART CHERRY CRUMBLE

Mario Batali is an award-winning chef and co-owner of numerous restaurants worldwide, the most notable of which is Babbo in New York City. Mario is the author of nine cookbooks, including the James Beard Award-winning *Molto Italiano: 327 Simple Italian Recipes*. Mario appears daily on ABC's *The Chew*, a daytime talk show that celebrates and explores life through food.

Tart cherry crumbles are a blast of summer when you enjoy them warm on a cold, snowy winter day. Their success relies on the quality of cherries, and nothing makes me happier than Michigan's very own fine selection of cherries in season. If you don't have the luxury of fresh Michigan cherries, store-bought fruit or even a frozen variety will do just fine. Enjoy!

Time: One to two hours

Serves twelve

MAIN INGREDIENTS

- 1 store-bought or homemade pie dough
- 2 14-ounce jars tart cherries in juice (½ cup liquid reserved)
- 1 lemon (zest and juice)
- ½ cup sugar
- 1 tablespoon cornstarch

CRUMBLE INGREDIENTS

- ⅓ cup flour
- ⅓ cup quick-cooking oats
- ¼ cup Amaretti cookies
- 1 tablespoon brown sugar
- 4 tablespoons cold butter (cubed)
- Salt
- Powdered sugar (to garnish)
- Greek yogurt (to serve)

INSTRUCTIONS

1. Preheat oven to 375°F.

2. Roll pie dough to ⅛-inch thickness on a lightly floured surface. Place dough into a pie dish and line with parchment and baking beans.

3. Cook for ten minutes, then carefully remove baking beans and parchment. Continue to bake for seven to eight more minutes, or until bottom of crust is cooked and pale golden. Remove from oven and set aside.

4. Meanwhile, whisk together the cornstarch and reserved liquid in a large bowl.

5. Add the cherries, lemon zest, lemon juice, and sugar. Stir together, then transfer to the prepared crust.

Continued on page 22

6. Combine the crumble ingredients minus the butter in a food processor and pulse until cookie pieces are smaller than a pea. Add butter and pulse until butter is crumbled. Top cherries with the crumble and place pie into the oven for thirty to thirty-five minutes. Crumble topping should be a rich golden color.

7. Remove and allow to cool to room temperature. Serve with powdered sugar and greek yogurt.

HELPFUL TIPS

1. Mix the crumble ingredients well before adding butter so it doesn't cling to one ingredient in the mixture.

2. If you don't allow the pie to rest, the slices will not hold their shape.

KITCHENWARE

- Rolling pin
- Liquid measuring cup
- Measuring cup (set)
- Whisk
- Mixing bowl

Lucy Centeno

 Lucy Centeno is a *chiquita* of seventeen. She is from a small country named Honduras. She was born on December 13, 1995. She loves to be around her family and friends. There is nothing more important to her than her younger sister and brother. In her life she has been through difficult moments, but she has learned that if you know how to play in life, you will either learn how to win or how to lose. She is a fantastic, wonderful girl. She goes to Ypsilanti Community High School. When she is older, she wants to become a nurse or an undercover cop.

AGE 18

Recipe for *Tajadas con Pollo*

Tajadas con Pollo is this fantastic, delicious plate that is one of the main dishes in Honduras. You can make it any day or for any event you would like to. It might sound weird, or you might think it would taste nasty, but once you try it, you'll be like, "Wow! This is really tasty!"

Estimated time: One hour

INGREDIENTS

- Green bananas
- Chicken
- Cabbage
- Tomatoes
- Onions
- Green pepper
- *Consome de pollo*
- Flour
- Salt
- Mayonnaise

DIRECTIONS

1. First, peel the green bananas.
2. Clean the chicken and put the *consome de pollo* on it.
3. Chop the bananas in round, thin pieces and add a little bit of salt.
4. Put the chopped bananas in a pan to fry. Then take them out and put them on a plate.
5. Dip the chicken in the flour and put the chicken in the pan to fry.
6. To make the sauce, chop the onions, peppers, and tomatoes. Then blend all these together in a blender with water and salt.
7. For the salad, chop the cabbage in thin slices. If you would like, chop onions, tomatoes, and pepper, and add them. Add mayonnaise.
8. Finally, put the bananas on a plate. Serve as much as you want. Put the chicken on top. Then add the sauce and salad. You can add parmesan cheese if you would like.
9. Enjoy it!

La Aventura Hacia USA, or The Adventure to the USA

HI, MY NAME IS LUCIA, but I don't like that name, so I prefer that people call me Lucy. I was born in Honduras on September 13, 1995, but on my birth certificate it says I was born on December 13, 1995. When I was six years old, my mom came to the USA, and I stayed with my grandmother. I went to school over there until fifth grade.

Before coming to the USA, I remember I was in a Royal Competition. When it was time for votes, I dressed like a cowgirl and rode a horse. I was looking really pretty. I had to do my hair and make-up. My family helped me look really nice. That day we had a party; then, when they knew who won a week later, I had to go buy the dress, shoes, and crown, because I won the princess position. A few weeks later, we had a party. It was really weird and awesome. A month later, we were on a school break. My mom called and said we had to leave in that minute to come to the USA.

Coming to the USA was like an adventure to me. There was this one amazing, bright afternoon in August 2006. My sister, cousin, and I were playing in the backyard at Grandma's house when we heard the loud noise of the house phone ringing. My grandmother quickly got up and answered. I just remember seeing my sweet, beautiful, and gentle grandma start to cry. I didn't know it was my mother calling until my grandma said, "*Tu mami quiere hablar contigo.*" I got up from the floor where I was playing with dolls with my sister and cousin. I got the phone, and I said, "*Hola, Mami.*" My mother started to tell me to get some clothes ready because I was coming to the USA. So then I understood why my grandma was crying.

While my mother was talking, I was thinking, *How is this going to be?* I was excited to go with my mom, but at the same time I wasn't, because I didn't want to leave my family behind. They have always been with me in good or bad situations. But I had to leave them behind and come with my mother.

When everything was ready, my grandmother Lucia and my grandfather Toño took us to downtown Yoro—Yoro is in Honduras. We got on a bus that was yellow to go to my uncle's house in San Pedro Sula.

The trip was a little long and exhausting. I just remember seeing my grandmother crying all the way through the trip. I felt sad knowing that I was leaving them. Finally we got to the bus station in San Pedro Sula.

The stations in Honduras are not like big buildings, or even small buildings where you buy the tickets. It's more like a simple stop or parking lot where all the buses wait. You have to find where each bus is going and get on the one you want. While you are on your way, someone will pass through the bus to collect the amount of money you have to pay. So we got dropped in front of my uncle's house, and my grandparents dropped off my sister and me.

It was hard for us to say bye to our grandparents, but we had to. Then, later on the same day, my uncle Henry drove us to the border of Guatemala and Mexico. We had some rough times there with the couple who picked us up. They were friends of my ex-stepdad. I don't know how all these people knew where we were or who we were. All I know is that my mom talked to all of them on the phone.

A week later, we met with a white lady and her son to go to Texas. We got on a bus and went to her house. Later on, on a breezy, light night, they told me that they were taking us to be with my mom. I remember getting in this little old four-door car. After that I don't remember anything—until the next day when my little sister woke me up and said, "We're here! Look, there is Mom!"

So we got out of the car quickly, and I ran to my mom with my sister. I remember I was excited and I cried of happiness. My mom was looking so different from what I remembered she looked like. She was whiter and gained a little weight, but she was still looking beautiful and young as always. She had her black long hair and her soft cheeks. Reuniting with her was the best part of the trip, but also I felt this sadness and pain in my heart because of my lovely, enormous, and fantastic family that I left.

I finally got to meet my annoying, crazy little brother who I love a lot now. When he saw us he hit us. I was like, *What the heck?*, but I just let it go. I think in his mind he was like, *Who are these girls?*

So we got inside this green Toyota car my mom had. I could see in her eyes that she was happy and excited to have us with her again. We had a long trip to get to Tennessee, this calm, quiet place where I could feel it was going to be amazing to live and be with my mother. Then we got to my mom's house, a beautiful place where I knew I was going to be happy and where I would grow up. I still remember that wonderful morning on August 23, 2006, like it was yesterday.

Open Letter

Dear teacher,

I feel that in class we need to cooperate more. We should also have more security in class because students are grabbing things and having fights. I don't think that is right. Another thing is that the class is too crowded. I think we should have more teachers. We should have a class full of positive ideas, and we need to participate more. Those are some of the needs in the crowded, loud classrooms full of negative, rude students.

I think this is because we see too much drama going on with students. They don't really know how to behave. It's like their parents never taught them good manners. We students should encourage one another to be better and to do our best. Finally, there should be more attention for us from our teacher so each day we cooperate more and have a better classroom.

I advise you to ask each student what they have learned or what you have taught during the class time, or at least for us to share with teammates. You should be patient in teaching us and not get angry. Help us students to have a different attitude toward our elders and you teachers. There are ways that you can give us advice to become better. This is just what I think.

I hope you can encourage us students to love to work in class. For example, to make our class more vivid, or to have more ideas for how we can work as teammates. I think if you have ways to encourage us, we actually will put in more effort to get it. It will be more calm than loud and boring, because we students love to have classes where we can share and communicate with one another a lot.

Sincerely,

Lucy

Mindy Vu

 Mindy Vu was born in Pennsylvania. She enjoys playing Minecraft. She enjoys eating chicken noodle soup and fish. She would love to be a teacher. She loves to play Minecraft because it has diamonds.

AGE 8

Pen-pal Letters

Dear pen-pal,

My name is Mindy. My language is Vietnamese. My age is eight. My school is Adams STEM Academy. My teacher's name is Ms. S. My favorite book is *Itty-Bitty Animals*. My siblings are two sisters and one brother. What is your name? What is your favorite food? What language do you speak? What's your age? What is your favorite pet? How many siblings do you have?

Sincerely,

Mindy

Dear Mindy,

I'm glad I could write to you. My name is Lucy C. My favorite food is this Hispanic food called *tajadas con pollo*. This food is green fried bananas with fried chicken and has tomato sauce that we make, and also it has this salad of cabbage that we also make. I speak Spanish and English. I'm seventeen years old. My favorite pets are dogs. I also love dolphins. Here in the United States, I have a sister and a brother, but in Honduras I have another sister and brother, too. Is there anything else you would like to know about me? What do you want to be when you grow up? Do you play any sports or do you like any sports? What is your favorite subject in school? I'll be waiting for your response with joy.

Sincerely,

Lucy

Dear Lucy,

Yes, I would like to know more about you. When I grow up, I want to be a singer. I do not like any sports. My favorite subject in school is math. How are you doing? Do you have a job? What is your pet's name, or do you not have a pet? You write nice and pretty. What is your teacher's name? What do you do after school? What is your favorite holiday? My favorite holiday is Christmas. On Christmas morning, I open fifteen presents.

Sincerely,

Mindy

Dear Mindy,

It is really nice talking to you again. I'm really excited to be talking to you guys who are really young. Being a singer is a nice career. I also like singing. We've got things in common. My favorite subject is also math. I'm pretty good! How about you? Yes, I do have a job. I work in a restaurant by Briarwood Mall called Los Amigos. I do not have a pet, how about you? I have several teachers, but the one I like the most is Ms. Sirman. After school, I go straight to work. What do you do after school? I really don't have a favorite holiday; I only like the breaks we have during holidays while we are at school. You're lucky! You get more presents than I do. Is there anything else you would like to know about me? It's really nice talking to you.

Sincerely,

Lucy C.

....

Dear Lucy,

I sometimes have trouble in math. I also don't have a pet, too. When I was little, I had a pet fish, but it died. My brother named him Memo. After school my daddy picks me up and takes me to go to my babysitter's. How many friends do you have? How are your parents? On Christmas, how many presents do you get? My favorite food experience that I enjoy is Vietnamese food, like rice.

Sincerely,

Mindy

Dear Mindy,

I think if you practice math, you will get better each time. Sorry for that. I also used to have fish, but when I moved here we left them. So you spend time after school with your babysitter. I have a lot of friends, I can't count them. How about you? I only have my mother with me. My dad passed away. On Christmas, I only got a present from my mom. Since I'm older now, I have to work for my things. That's nice that you enjoy Vietnamese food. How does it taste? My favorite food is this Latino food called *tajadas con pollo*. It's fried green bananas or plantains with fried chicken, then we put a salad on top and some tomato sauce with parmesan cheese. It tastes so good.

Sincerely,

Lucy

....

Dear Lucy,

I have a little group of friends. I don't have a lot of friends because in my classroom there are a lot of boys and they're bullies. My spaghetti tastes wonderful. What kind of TV shows do you like? What kind of animals do you want? How is your school like a family? My teacher Ms. S., always helps me do my work in class.

Sincerely,

Mindy V.

Jasmil De La Cruz-Ramirez

Jasmil De La Cruz-Ramirez was born in the Dominican Republic in 1997. Until 2013, she went to N.S.P.S., a military school in the Dominican Republic. She is now a student at Ypsilanti Community High School because she moved to Michigan, where she lives with her father, Leonardo De La Cruz Perez. Her mother, Dolores Maria Ramirez, still lives in the DR. She misses her mom a lot. Jasmil likes going to church and misses it since coming to Michigan. She also likes talking on the phone with her mom and her friends for hours at a time. Horatio of *CSI Miami* is her favorite TV character. Jasmil wants to be a successful psychologist because she likes to help people solve their problems. Since she was a little girl, her friends have been asking her for help.

AGE 17

Recipe for *Yaroa*

When I eat this food, I feel so good because this has a delicious flavor. The ketchup, meat, cheese, and mayonnaise flavors are an amazing combination in my mouth. You can make this food anywhere and eat it with your family and friends. In my country, the people love this food. This food is Dominican, and the Dominican Republic has a lot of fields and a few cities. Santiago is the city where the *yaroa* is from. The people go there to try the best *yaroa*, but you can eat it in other places, too.

Estimated time: Ten minutes

INGREDIENTS

- French fries (in the pot)
- Beef or chicken (in the pot)
- Ketchup
- Mayonnaise
- Cheese
- Vegetables, whatever ones you like, cut up with a knife
- Oil
- *Aji* (chile pepper)

DIRECTIONS

1. Fry potatoes in the pot.
2. Cut the vegetables, whatever ones you like. For example: tomatoes, *aji*, onions . . .
3. Cook the meat with onion, oil, *aji*, however you like your meat done.
4. Put the french fries in a bowl. On the french fries, you put the meat and the ketchup, mayonnaise, cheese, and vegetables.

A Little Part of My Life

WHEN I WAS IN THE DOMINICAN REPUBLIC, I went every weekend to my cousin's home. We went to the movie theater with my little cousin Rosa and my aunt Sandra; we enjoyed that. We are a united family.

After the movie theater, we went to eat something like pizza or Burger King, and then we played games at the mall. I have a pretty strong bond with my family.

My favorite store in the Dominican Republic is Zara, because that store has all I want. It is big, and they have good prices for me. The movie theater in the Dominican Republic is small, but in the Blue Mall, the movie theater is bigger. I love that movie theater, because when I would go with my friends, we played around and that was funny.

Then, when I was getting to my house, I knew that my mom was cooking my favorite food, because I could smell it around the house. She was cooking rice, beef, *gandules*, and green salad with avocado. I love it when I smell this food; I feel a lot of happiness.

Open Letter

Dear school board,

I have some ideas to make the school a stronger community. I think the school needs better food, because the food is not good, and the cafeteria needs to be cleaner. There needs to be more healthy food.

I think the school needs more security, because the teenagers smoke outside of the school. I don't like to wear a lot of clothes in the high school, but the high school doesn't have enough heating so I have to wear a lot of clothes.

I think the school should suspend students for being disrespectful to teachers.

I think the school has good areas, hours, and good teachers.

I'd like more activities, like a party for Valentine's Day, and more field trips, and more security guards who take their jobs seriously.

I hope to help the school if they take my ideas to make improvements.

From,

Jasmil De La Cruz-Ramirez

Pen-pal Letters

Dear Mindy,

Nice name. My name is Jasmil. My language is Spanish. My age is seventeen. My birthday is on January 13. My school is Ypsilanti Community High School. My teacher is Ms. Sirman. She's cute. I have one brother, his age is thirteen, and a little sister who is eight. My favorite food is lasagna. My favorite pet is a Yorkshire Terrier (this is a small, pretty dog). In my country I have a lot of friends, but here I don't. I have a few friends. I'm from the Dominican Republic. It's amazing. When I was little I had a pet fish too, but it died. On Christmas, I had five presents, not much. I have troubles in math, too. Well, Mindy, I can see we have many things in common. You are very cute, Mindy, nice to meet you.

Jasmil

Dear Jasmil,

Nice to meet you. I'm the same age as your little sister. My teacher's name is Mrs. S. My teacher's name is hard to spell. What is your sister's name and your brother's name? What do your friends like to do? How's your teacher? What color is your dog's collar? What's your favorite snack? Well, it's nice talking to you. Talk to you later!

Sincerely,

Mindy

....

Dear Mindy,

It's nice to meet you, too. That is so cute that you and my little sister are the same age. She would like to meet you also. You have learned the name of your teacher fast. You are very smart, don't worry about that. My sister's name is Greisy and my brother's name is Leo. What is your favorite snack? Well, my friends like to eat a lot of foods: pizza, hamburgers, rice, meat, snacks, and other foods. My teacher is very beautiful. She's blonde, she has beautiful hazel-colored eyes. I love my teacher because she helps me with my homework and she teaches me English, too. I don't have a dog right now, I'm sorry. Do you have a dog? What do you like to do on weekends? My favorite snack is Cheddar Cheese Lays. Well, I would like to meet you soon.

Sincerely,

Jasmil

SIMPLE KALE PIE AND CANTALOUPE CREAMSICLE

Annie Elder is a head farmer at the Community Farm of Ann Arbor, which is based on both the biodynamic and the community-supported agriculture (CSA) models. The Community Farm, operating since 1988, is the oldest CSA in Michigan and the eighth-oldest in the country. With full-time farmers Paul Bantle and Annie Elder, apprentices, and help from many members, the Community Farm of Ann Arbor grows produce for 180 members and their families.

SIMPLE KALE PIE

This recipe is fun because you can tweak it into many different variations. You can substitute quinoa or millet for the rice. You can vary your cheese type. You can use Swiss chard or another green. It pretty much always comes out good.

- 1 ½ cups cooked rice
- 2 eggs
- 1 ½ cups milk (any kind: cow, rice, soy, etc.)
- 1 cup grated cheese
- 1 teaspoon salt
- 4 large kale leaves

INSTRUCTIONS

1. Spread the rice evenly in a pie pan, including on the sides.
2. Whisk eggs.
3. Add milk to the eggs and whisk in a big bowl.
4. Mince kale into small pieces.
5. Combine kale, cheese, salt, and milk-egg mixture.
6. Pour into pie shell.
7. Bake at 350°F for forty-five minutes or until center is firm.

CANTALOUPE CREAMSICLE

Maybe you don't love cantaloupe, but you're sure to love this summer treat, especially on a very hot day. In a blender or food processor, combine all ingredients. Blend up until very smooth.

- 2 cups chopped up, cantaloupe
- 1 cup vanilla ice cream
- ⅛ teaspoon salt

Carlos De La Rosa

Carlos J. De La Rosa was born in 1996, on November 6. Carlos has a big future ahead of him, but he doesn't know that. He is only seventeen years old. He goes to Ypsilanti Community High School. Carlos doesn't have a lot of friends, but he doesn't need friends to get through life. He is from the Dominican Republic. He really likes to play sports, loves his mother, and he also loves God.

AGE 17

How to Change a Tire on the Middle of the Highway or Road

Imagine you are alone in the middle of the road with a flat tire and you are on your way to school to take a really important test. Cars are flying by you while you are pulled over. You could encounter serious injury just while waiting for someone to come help you change your tire. Don't you want to do this all on your own and get out of there without all this happening to you? Here are the steps to fix this problem quickly and safely, and it can also help you save money.

Estimated time: It depends

MATERIALS

- Car
- A jack
- A tire
- Socket wrench (looks like this: +)
- Flashlight (optional)

DIRECTIONS

1. How to change a flat tire is really simple. First, you will notice you have a flat tire when the car has a lean to either side, or you can hear a tire flopping, or the steering wheel starts shaking a lot.

2. Second, you want to find a parking area or move to the side of the road, but try to find a parking area just to be safe.

3. Now that you're safe and want to solve the problem, you need to start getting your tools out and not get freaked out.

4. Put the jack under the car, right in front of the front door on the chassis, or the frame of the car (because if you put it anywhere else you could flip the car or not lift the car at all).

5. You know the car is fully jacked when the tire is off the ground. The jack you could even do with one hand because it is so easy.

6. After you lift the car, you loosen the bolts with the socket wrench. Try out all four sides to find the size of the bolts (every car is different). Remove all the bolts.

7. Grab the flat tire, pull it out, and put it to the side. Grab the donut, or spare, and push it into place (make sure you don't get your fingers caught, because if you get a finger caught, you might not get it back). Screw the bolts back in.

8. Now you have to unjack the car. If you twist the jack to your left, it should start coming down (the car and the jack).

9. Put the flat back in the trunk so you can go get it fixed later. Get it fixed as fast as you can, because driving on a donut is dangerous. It is thinner than a regular tire—you're basically driving with three-and-a-half wheels.

A Really Big Future

THIS IS THE LIFE OF A KID who has a really big future. His name is Carlos Javier Diaz De La Rosa. He was born on November 6, 1996. He was born in the Dominican Republic in the city of Los Arcarzob.

The kid grew up in San Cristobal Palenque. It is a really poor side of the country. Where this kid grew up, all he had was his grandmother and grandfather, but he never asked where his mom or his dad were. When Carlos was five, he started taking school more seriously. He learned how to read at the age of seven.

It was Monday at 7:40AM. Carlos woke up and got ready for school. On his way to school, he saw a lot of baseball players practicing on a baseball field, and he thought, *Why aren't those kids at school?* The week went past, and it was Saturday morning. One of Carlos' friends went to his house and asked Carlos if he wanted to go to the baseball field with him.

Carlos was at the baseball field with his friend; for the moment, he was watching his friend practice. The coach called Carlos and told him to help him by catching the ball for him. After three Saturdays, Carlos was still going to his friend's practice. It was game day, and Carlos was in the locker room with all the players and his friend, but there was one thing that Carlos had to ask himself: *Why am I not on this team?*

After the game was over, Carlos asked the coach if he could play for them, but there was a problem. Carlos came from a really poor family, so he didn't have a lot. Carlos had to pay 15,000 pesos in order to be able to play and go to other countries with the team. Carlos was sad about not having the money to play baseball, so Carlos started working hard to make money and working to become a good ball player. After three months, Carlos went to practice and he practiced like he never had. Carlos was so good that the coach pulled him aside and told him not to worry about the 15,000 pesos, that he was going to pay it. Carlos dropped down to his knees and said, "Thank you, God," and he said thank you to the coach and gave him a hug.

My First Love (Echo)

I WAS EXCITED, BUT AT THE SAME TIME I felt nervous about how things were going to go at my first day of school. I was in my house getting ready to catch the bus to go to school in the United States for the first time. My brother was also going to school with me, but he was going to high school and I was going to middle school. Before I left the house, my mom said that I had to eat, but I didn't want to.

I was waiting for the school bus when it finally got there. There were a lot of people inside the bus. I finally found a seat next to a girl who was really friendly. The girl started talking to me, but I didn't understand what she was asking me or telling me; all I knew how to say was "yes."

On my way to school I saw a lot of things I had never seen before: I saw a deer on the side of the road and a lot of other amazing things. I finally got to school and I could not believe it; I thought I was in the wrong place for a minute. I walked inside a big building and I thought I was never going to find the way to my classes, but Amanda, the first person who talked to me on the bus, took me to my first class. I was shy for some reason, but I was calm at the same time. The teacher asked me to tell my name to the class. All I understood was "name" so I just said it to the class.

The class was over, so the bell rang, but I did not know what it was. Everybody got up and walked out of the class, but I did not. The teacher came over to ask me about my next class, but I really did not know what she was asking or saying to me.

So I was finally in my second hour, but I was the last one to get in the classroom. I saw someone I knew—there she was again: Amanda. Amanda was starting to catch my eye; she was a really beautiful girl, too. I, of course, sat down right next to her. I was loving school so far. It was time for me to go back on the bus to go back home and tell my mom how my first day in school was. I didn't know how to get out to catch the bus outside, but there she was again. The most beautiful girl I had seen. Amanda took me to the bus with her, and we were headed home on a beautiful, sunny day.

Amanda was beautiful, smart, and cute. Her hair was blonde; she was a white girl. Her eyes were blue like the ocean, and they were the most beautiful eyes I have ever seen. I was thinking that she was going to be mean at first, because she was sitting at the back of the bus on a seat all by herself, but she turned out to be the most cute girl I had ever met. I had to walk through a lot of people to get to her seat on the bus. It all turned out great because she was my first friend and my first love.

Open Letter

Dear YCHS,

I have some suggestions for improving the school. We are in need of more books, because some classes have way too many people, and a lot of students don't get to use books. We also need more cleaning staff to keep our school looking presentable. The rules in our school are made, but nobody is following them the way they should be. More counselors will also help this school become a better place to be in, and students will be more prepared to go out in the real world.

I am the best person to write this personal letter to YCHS because I am a student in the YCS district. I can see what the school needs, because I have been here for two years and I have gone through all of these things.

I have suggestions that could help all the needs become reality. Fundraising could really help to buy more books for students who need them.

The rules are there, but people are not following them well enough, and they are not being punished enough for what they are doing. We need to get more counseling going, and for that we can start training more teachers to become counselors.

The thing that the school is doing right is trying to make the changes. This school also has great teachers who really want to help us succeed. We also have a lot of volunteers who come in and help us with things that we will really need in the future. There is also really good security who get things done around the school. The size of the school is great to be around.

From,

Carlos

Ali Doumbouya

Ali Doumbouya was born in the south side of Ypsilanti. He enjoys watching basketball. Ali's favorite food is corn dogs. Ali's mom and dad were born in West Africa. Ali's favorite basketball player is Lebron James. Ali is good at shooting three-pointers. When he grows up, he wants to be a lawyer.

AGE 8

....

Recipe for Chocolate Waffles

INGREDIENTS

- Chocolate waffles
- Syrup
- Plate
- Microwave

DIRECTIONS

1. Buy chocolate waffles from Sam's Club.
2. Put them on a plate.
3. Put the plate in the microwave.
4. Put it in for two minutes.
5. Take it out with a napkin.
6. Cover the waffles with syrup.

Pen-pal Letters

Dear pen-pal,

My name is Ali. I speak Mandingo. My age is eight. I am in third grade. My favorite sport is basketball. My favorite candy is Mike and Ikes. My height is 3.8 feet. What grade are you in? What's your name? Do you play for a basketball team? Where are you from? What is your teacher's name? What is your favorite movie?

From,

Ali

Dear pen-pal Ali,

My name is Carlos Javier De La Rosa. I speak three languages: Spanish, English, and Portuguese. I am in twelfth grade, the last year of high school. My favorite sports are baseball and soccer. My height is 5'11". My teacher's name is Ms. Sirman. My favorite movie is *Radio*. I am from the Dominican Republic. I have a big brother. What specific place in Africa are you from?

From,

Carlos

....

Dear Carlos,

I am from the west side of Africa. My grandma lives in Africa. My grandpa died, but I still have family members in Africa. I am going to Africa and New York in the summer. I celebrate Eid. Eid is when fathers, uncles, grandpas, and grandmas give kids money. What holiday do you celebrate? Do you have family in Dominican? Are you good at baseball?

From,

Ali

Dear Ali,

I don't really have any holiday that I celebrate. I have all of my family in the Dominican Republic. I guess that I could say that I'm good at basketball. When are you going to Africa and New York? I am going to the Dominican Republic in the summer with my mom and my brother. My grandparents are both alive, and they are also in the Dominican Republic. What languages do you speak? What do you like to do in your free time?

From,

Carlos

....

Dear Carlos,

I speak Mandingo and English. I am going to Africa in three more years because my dad is not that good at speaking English, so they will have to get a translator. But I'm going to New York in the summer on a subway. How long are you staying in Dominican? What do you plan on doing there? I go out to eat at the Chinese buffet. My favorite thing to get there is shrimp. Did you ever go to the Chinese buffet?

From,

Ali

....

Dear Ali,

I will stay in the Dominican Republic for my high school vacation. I love going to the Chinese buffet.

From,

Carlos

Dear Carlos,

A thing that is challenging is science because I do not know any experiments. Adams STEM Academy is like a family because everybody knows everybody. My classmates are like brothers and sisters. We have school laws. How is your school like a family?

From,

Ali

....

Dear Ali,

Something challenging for me is one of my high school classes, which is called ELL. My family is really big, but none of them are in here in the United States. My classmates are not really my family, because I don't really know them as much.

From,

Carlos

....

To Carlos,

I play for a team called YMCA. I'm supposed to play with the three and four but they moved me up with the five and six. What is your favorite channel? What is one of your recipes? What is your school like?

From,

Ali

FRANK FEJERAN

PRESENTS

RED ONION MARMALADE

Frank Fejeran is an Ann Arbor native and
the Executive Chef of Ravens Club,
a restaurant and jazz club in downtown Ann
Arbor. After spending time in Escondido,
California, Chicago, Illinois, and Farmington Hills,
Michigan, Frank returned to Ann Arbor in 2009 to
bring everything he learned about food
and cooking local to his hometown.

This recipe is the very first recipe I was shown by my mentor chef, Riko Bartolome. The man has taught me an immense amount about cooking, passion, dedication, and life. Every time I make this recipe, I can see him and hear him. I feel like an eighteen-year-old *commis* again. The marmalade is a constant reminder of why I began this career and why I have put so much toward it. It goes on the menu in some form, on every menu I create.

The reason this recipe is so special is because you are taking such a humble ingredient, the onion, and turning it into an amazing, versatile experience; there's nothing like it. That is one of the main reasons chefs are chefs: creating and transforming ingredients into something spectacular. This marmalade can go on a burger (as it does at The Ravens Club), or can be served with cheese or chicken liver mousse, or simply spread on a slice of toast. The most important part of the recipe that follows is patience.

MAIN INGREDIENTS

- 10 red onions, shaved thin
- 1 cup sugar
- 3 cups red wine
- ½ cup red wine vinegar
- 1 cup honey
- 5 cups chicken stock

SACHET INGREDIENTS

- 1 cinnamon stick
- A bunch of thyme
- 5 cloves
- A pinch of peppercorns

DIRECTIONS

1. Sweat the onions until broken down a touch in a spot of oil.

2. Once wilted, add in sugar, wine, vinegar, honey, and sachet, and bring to a boil.

3. Simmer until reduced by a third.

4. Add stock, and cover and reduce until it turns thick and syrupy.

5. Remove the sachet and cool.

Babacar Diallo

 Babacar Diallo was born in Conakry, Guinea, in 1996. He grew up with grandparents and aunts and uncles. He played soccer with his friends and in a club. Babacar moved to Michigan when he was eleven years old. He started learning English and played soccer for the school teams. He can play any position the team needs him to play. He loves to read and go to school every day. He dreams about being a good person and a professional soccer player. Sometimes the dream makes him cry. That's why he wants to play soccer.

AGE 17

How to Make a Hamburger

I like to eat a hamburger when I get hungry because hamburgers taste good. So sometimes I like to make a hamburger and to add ketchup.

Estimated time: One hour

MATERIALS

- 4 1-pound ground beef patties
- 4 hamburger buns
- 4 slices of cheese
- 4 leaves of lettuce
- 4 slices of onion
- 4 slices of tomato
- Ketchup
- Mustard
- Ranch salad dressing

DIRECTIONS

1. Preheat the oven to 350°F.
2. Put the patties on a tray, and put them in the oven. Cook for forty minutes. Turn them after twenty minutes.
3. Put the cooked burgers on a large plate with a fork.
4. Put a bottom hamburger bun on four different plates.
5. Put a slice of cheese on each bun.
6. Put one burger on top of the cheese.
7. Add the ketchup, mustard, and ranch dressing to taste.
8. Put one slice of lettuce, onion, and tomato on top of each burger.
9. Put the top bun on each burger.
10. Cut one hamburger in half for sister, Hadja.
11. Sit at the table, eat, and enjoy!

A Future Professional, like Cristiano Ronaldo, Ronaldinho Gaúcho, and Ricardo Kaká

I WAS BORN IN CONAKRY, GUINEA, on January 19, 1996. I spoke Fulani and French. I liked to go to school and play soccer. I was one of the best players on the team. I started playing soccer in the street and playing one-on-one.

The first game of my life I scored three goals, and I started thinking that I was a good soccer player. When I played soccer in the club FCA Bordeaux, I wore my jersey and shoes every day. Once, I missed the first part of a game because I was washing my clothes at home. They were losing 3-2, but my brother drove me to the game. Two minutes before the game was over, my friend Deko passed me the ball. I took a shot at the goal. I scored the goal. All my teammates were very happy that I made the score 3-3. It was an amazing goal because I was a little bit far to take the shot. The ball went right by the defense. I was very, very successful. We tied 3-3. We played again and I scored two more goals. We beat them 5-3. Then we were able to go to the final.

My teammates really liked me. They gave me my soccer team picture to remember my team and my country. They told me to always be good and do good in school to make my life better. They said, "Always keep playing because we know you are good." They told me to be a professional soccer player. I think about it and know they are right. I earned my nickname "Adriano," who is a professional player for Brazil. I have won ten championships from playing soccer in Guinea.

I moved to the United States in 2007, when I was eleven years old. Sometimes I visited my family in France. I first lived in Detroit. My school was called Thomas Middle School. I met my first girlfriend, who was named Jada. I also played soccer. When I moved to Ypsi, I also visited my auntie in New York City, in a place called Tin Town. I learned English in Ypsi. I ran track in Ypsi at East Middle School, and we won one year. I started to play football this year. I work so hard to play soccer because I want to be professional. It is why I am a nice man and a success.

Open Letter

Dear teachers and coaches,

Ypsilanti Community High is a good school, but we need to work together. We need teachers to help the students to get better in life because it is good for everybody. Students need to be respectful.

I am a hard worker in school. I take school very seriously. I know school is very important. I like to do homework because it helps me to get better in life. Teachers need to organize with students in school to get better. Teachers need to help students to do homework because it is good for them. The students need to collaborate, because you learn more things, and it is more fun. I hope that the teachers work hard so that students are more successful in school.

Thank you,

Babacar Diallo

Brian Chanthathirath

 Brian was born in Ypsilanti, Michigan. Brian speaks Laotian and English. His favorite foods are chicken and ribs. Brian's favorite things to do are making crafts, drawing, and painting. Brian wants to be a doctor when he grows up. Brian likes helping with cooking for his parents.

AGE 10

Recipe for Nachos

INGREDIENTS

- Tortilla chips
- Cheese
- Meat

DIRECTIONS

1. Buy a bag of tortilla chips, and open it and pour the chips in the bowl.

2. Melt cheese in the microwave for one minute. When it's done take it out.

3. Pour the cheese on the tortilla chips.

4. Cook the meat, and when you're done, pour it on the tortilla chips.

5. You're done! Invite friends and family.

Pen-pal Letters

Dear pen-pal,

I like to play soccer because it is good for my life. I am very personal and successful in sports. I am from Guinea. I speak French and English. My name is Babacar Diallo. Where do you come from?

From,

Babacar Diallo

Dear Babacar,

My name is Brian. I was born in Michigan. I live in Michigan. I am ten years old. I would like to meet you. I speak Laotian. That's where my family came from. I am in fourth grade. What grade are you in? Have you ever traveled anywhere? I traveled to California and Las Vegas. Do you have a pet? I have a dog. My tradition, we just dance and party for New Year's. Do you have a tradition? Can't wait to see your next letter!

P.S. How old are you?

Sincerely,

Brian

....

Dear Brian,

I am in twelfth grade. I have traveled to DC and New York. I have a dog in Guinea. My girlfriend gives me presents. I am seventeen years old.

From,

Babacar Diallo

Dear Babacar,

Who is your favorite singer? My favorite singer is Bruno Mars. Also, what is your favorite season? My favorite season is summer. And what is your favorite food? My favorite food is *pho*. It is a popular Vietnamese noodle soup. What is your favorite food? And what is your favorite restaurant or buffet? My favorite buffet is Hibachi Grill. Can't wait to see your next letter.

Sincerely,

Brian

....

Dear Babacar,

My school is very fun. My favorite subjects are writing, drawing, and playing with my friends. My friends feel like they're my cousins because they're nice to me, and they make me laugh. How is your school like a family? Also, every summer I go to California.

Sincerely,

Brian

....

Dear Brian,

Ypsilanti High School is very good and fun. We have a lot of different people. I like soccer, track, and football at school. My favorite class is history because I like to listen to the stories about fighting. Sometimes my friends and I laugh. Do you have fun in California in the summer?

Best wishes,

Babacar Diallo

NOAH GOLDSMITH

PRESENTS

BELGIAN WAFEL WITH MAPLE GLAZE

Noah Goldsmith is the founder and owner of The Wafel Shop, a cafe in downtown Ann Arbor serving creative and authentic Belgian wafels. He has an MBA in marketing and finance from Wayne State University. Noah worked for Zingerman's Deli in Ann Arbor during high school, and continued working there through college; this first job started a passion for food and stringent standards for service.

I have been a lifelong fan of waffles. When I was young, my grandmother would take me to our local diner every Saturday, and I would always have a Belgian waffle with butter and syrup. In college, I had my first taste of authentic European waffles while studying abroad, which is where the idea for The Wafel Shop came from ('wafel' is the Dutch spelling). To me, wafels are a blank canvas to create a breakfast masterpiece!

With that in mind, I want to share a recipe that reminds me of my grandmother—on holidays, she would make a carrot cake with an amazing maple glaze. I have found that this glaze goes great over our wafels. This combination also goes well with berries, chocolate, and whipped cream. I encourage you to make your own wafel masterpiece!

BELGIAN WAFEL INGREDIENTS

- 2 eggs
- 2 cups all-purpose flour
- 1 ¾ cups whole milk
- ½ cup vegetable oil
- 1 tablespoon sugar
- 1 teaspoon kosher salt
- 1 tablespoon baking powder
- ½ teaspoon vanilla extract (optional)

MAPLE GLAZE INGREDIENTS

- ⅓ cup of Grade A maple syrup
- 1 tablespoon unsalted butter (room temperature)
- 1 ¼ cups powdered (confectioners') sugar
- ½ teaspoon cinnamon
- 1 teaspoon vanilla

EQUIPMENT

- Hand-mixer, stand-mixer, or whisk
- Waffle iron
- Note: Not all waffle irons are alike—cook times and portion size will vary.

MAPLE GLAZE DIRECTIONS

1. Combine maple glaze ingredients in a mixing bowl.

2. Whisk ingredients together until a smooth consistency is achieved.

3. Set aside until ready to serve.

BELGIAN WAFEL DIRECTIONS

1. Combine wet and dry ingredients in a mixing bowl.

2. Mix ingredients together until there are no visible lumps.

3. Heat your waffle iron at the highest setting.

4. Ladle batter into the heated iron and quickly close the lid.

5. Cook the wafel until the exterior has developed a golden brown color, three to three-and-a-half minutes.

6. Carefully remove the wafel from the iron.

7. Drizzle the maple glaze over the wafel, and enjoy!

Ivan Gonzalez-Acevedo

 Ivan Gonzalez-Acevedo was born in Michoacan, Mexico, on September 4, 1996. He is a seventeen-year-old who likes to listen to music. He comes from a really poor and humble family. He goes to YCHS. He enjoys hanging out with his friends. Ivan also likes to drive around. He hopes to grow up to be a successful person and to be a role model among his family.

AGE 17

How to Make *La Posada* or a Mexican Christmas Evening Party

Christmas is a time of happiness, and there's no better way to be happy than to party. When you party, you forget about your problems and you just let go. A *Posada* is full of happiness and cheerful feelings. If you haven't been in a *Posada*, you haven't lived.

Estimated time: Eight hours (a long time)

MATERIALS

- 3-5 different homes
- Candy
- *Ponche* (punch)
- Hot chocolate
- Treats

- Tamales
- Beans
- Rice
- Tortillas
- Mexican music and holiday songs in Spanish

- Beer for the adults
- 2-3 *piñatas*, with the seven-cone star design (just one isn't enough)
- Kids dressed up as angels

DIRECTIONS

1. Dress up nicely, then get together with the rest of the people to start *la Posada*. (By this time, the last house where *la Posada* is going to be at should be ready and set.)

2. Sing along with the people to see if it's the house for the party and walk with them to the first house.

3. Sing outside the house, asking if it's the right house for *la Posada*, until people sing that it's not the right house and then move along.

4. Go to two or three more houses and sing, and then get the people from the house.

5. When you finally get to the house where the party is at, you sing and then eat.

6. Then you can dance and break *la piñata*.

7. Everything is organized by the community. In the party, there are neighbors, family members, and strangers.

English was my Weakness

I T HAD BEEN A WEEK OR TWO since we had arrived in the US. During this time, I didn't leave the house. When my mom told me I was going to school, I got excited but also worried because I didn't know any English yet. My mom bought me a backpack and school utensils. On Monday morning I woke up feeling weird. I got off the couch; yes, a couch. I folded my blanket and put it away in the closet. I hurried and brushed my teeth. My mom had already been awake since she worked almost all day and barely had time to sleep. She had already started the car, so I had no time to get breakfast.

On the way to the bus stop, I didn't talk. When we got to the bus stop, I was sad because I didn't want to get on the bus. There was some fog, therefore I couldn't see far. Two other girls waited for the bus as well. I didn't talk to them. When the bus finally arrived, I waited for the two girls to get on the bus. I finally got on the bus. I sat alone because I have always preferred being alone. On the bus all I could think about was how school was going to be. The bus made several stops to pick up students. I was so concentrated on my thinking that I didn't realize we had arrived at a school. Students started to get off and I decided to get off too.

When I got off the bus, I felt lost. I saw people walking different ways and I tried to follow them but then I saw others going another way so I followed, but I got nowhere. I felt frustrated. I tried talking to them but I didn't understand them and they didn't understand me. I felt like collapsing to the ground, when suddenly a hand grabbed my shoulder from behind. It was one of the girls who was at the bus stop earlier; her name was Dulce (candy). She took me back to the bus. We talked until we got to the school. Anguelina, the other girl, was also talking to me. They both gave me a tour around the school and helped me to get to my classes. They were sweet and funny. They became my friends.

Open Letter

Dear administration,

I have some ideas for making our school a better community. The school needs more efficient working security. To be able to have these new security guards, the school would need more money. The school could raise a good amount of money by having a café inside the school. With this extra money, the school could add more professional teachers and add more programs.

I have been a student at this high school for three years, therefore I'm a good person to advise you. I've been to different schools, so I have a pretty good idea of what works with students and what doesn't. I have friends who go to different high schools, and they tell me how theirs are different than mine.

Some ways the school can raise money are applying for grants with the help of teachers and students. An in-school café could be added to the school, which would give the school the money that is needed. The students could run the café as part of a marketing class.

You have done a great job in spending the money on this amazing technology. Items such as the Macs help students get work done faster. The security we have now does a good job, but with more security in the hallways, I—and everyone else—would feel safer.

I hope that in the near future this school will have the funds to provide a safer environment for the students and provide better technology to help them learn and graduate!

Sincerely,

Ivan Gonzalez-Acevedo

Mohamed Diane

 Mohamed Diane was born in Ypsilanti. Mohamed likes to play basketball. Mohamed likes to shoot hoops for fun. He wants to be a basketball player. He speaks Mandingo and English.

AGE 10

Pen-pal Letters

Dear pen-pal,

My name is Mohamed. Losany is my cousin. My favorite animal is a grizzly bear. My favorite movie is *Friday*. My favorite basketball team is the Miami Heat. Do you like M&Ms? What's your name? Can I get $2 when you send me a letter? You rock! Send it in an envelope. It was my birthday November 19. Bye-bye. Don't forget to send me money!

From,

Mohamed

Dear Mohamed,

My name is Ivan. I am from Mexico. I like monkeys. I love the movie *Friday*. I don't have a favorite basketball team. I like M&Ms. If you give me $5, I will give you $2. AND HAPPY LATE BIRTHDAY! How tall are you? I'm 5'5". What's your favorite food? I like pizza. Where are you from? Do you speak Mandingo? Do you play video games? How do you write "hey" in Mandingo? Write back or else! (JK.)

Sincerely,

Ivan Gonzalez

....

Dear Ivan,

Thanks for your letter. My favorite food is pizza, too. I'm from West Africa. I speak Mandingo. This is how you spell "hi" in my language: *cavath*. How do you say "hi" in your language? I have an Xbox One. I celebrate Eid. What do you celebrate? My Eid tradition is, we kill a lamb and give some to people. I love my tradition. What is yours? Please send me just $2, and I promise to give you $5 because I want to get this cool yo-yo. And if you can't give me me $2 for a yo-yo, please write me back. Don't get sick! Sorry I was sick, but I wanted to ask you, do you eat lamb? I hope you have a good Christmas and a happy New Year.

Sincerely,

Mohamed

Dear Mohamed,

This is Ivan. I don't eat lamb. I'm Mexican, and I don't know what Eid is. I had an amazing New Year's. How are you doing in school? How much money do you have? What do your parents work on? What's your favorite TV show? I celebrate Christmas. You say *hola* in Spanish, not "hi." I am from Southeast Mexico. I want the Xbox One. Sorry buddy, I'm broke. I don't have money. I don't want to get sick. I hope you don't get sick. I'm seventeen. How old are you? Have nice holidays!

Sincerely,

Ivan

Hi Ivan,

It's Mohamed. I went to a Mexican store. I don't remember the name. It is yellow, and they sell Takis. Lamb is good. My school's very fun. My favorite subject is pen-pals. I can make my school like a family by being nice. How is your school like a family?

Sincerely,

Mohamed

Dear Mohamed,

The Mexican store you went to is called Dos Hermanos Market. I used to work there for a summer. I love Takis. I'm pretty sure I wouldn't enjoy lamb. My school is really fun. I have many friends. My favorite subject in school is math. My family is not okay, but I'm still happy.

I started working about three weeks ago at Panda Express. It's fun working there. I get to eat whatever I want, whenever I want to. My life is coming to a turning point. I'm planning on moving out from my parents'. I already know where to go.

When I came to school today, I was walking in the hallways and I found a dollar on the floor. Since you once asked me for money I thought it would be nice if I gave it to you.

Sincerely,

Ivan Gonzalez

BRAD GREENHILL

PRESENTS

HOT CHEESE: JUST-MADE-MOZZARELLA, GARLIC CONFIT, CHARRED BREAD

Brad Greenhill is the chef and owner of Righteous Rojo, a pop-up restaurant operating in Detroit and Ann Arbor. While working at Carmen in Boston, Brad's cuisine was featured in *The New York Times. Bon Appetit*, and *Gourmet*. Brad's cooking continues to draw praise at community dinners across Metro Detroit. He plans to open a restaurant in Detroit in the near future.

Who doesn't love hot cheese?! Melty, gooey, glorious cheese! This dish was the first course at the first official pop-up dinner I ever did, back in April of 2011 at the Jefferson Market in Ann Arbor, Michigan. It's a dish that in many ways has been a lifetime in the making.

The initial concept came years ago during my tenure at Carmen Restaurant in Boston's North End. At Carmen, we used to make fresh mozzarella almost daily for a variety of items on the menu. At the end of any good mozzarella stretching session there would inevitably (read: purposely) be a bit of hot curd left over; not quite significant enough to make a proper ball for service, but coincidently the perfect amount for a cook's snack. Sprinkling the hot cheese with salt and a drizzle of olive oil was always a quick and delicious treat. On slower days, I'd take the snack a step further and wrap it in prosciutto slices with whole grain mustard or dip it in tomato sauce. However, most frequently, I found myself taking a piece of bread, slathering it with smashed garlic confit, and throwing it in the oven. It always bothered me that the mozzarella never had a starring role on the menu, and I thought it would be great to serve the mozzarella hot, pulled right out of the stretching liquid with a side of toasted garlic bread or other accoutrements.

While the idea was shaped in Boston, the inspiration came years later and is squarely rooted in childhood memories. It is the nostalgic flavor of the tin foil-bagged garlic bread served alongside Mom's heaping portions of buttered spaghetti with tomato sauce, found on almost any given night at the Greenhill household. It's the intoxicating smell of post-little-league-game outings at Pizza Hut, where drinking bottomless, frosted-red glasses of soda until your bladder screams uncle, and insisting your brother and his friends eat a mouthful of the red pepper flakes seemed like perfectly acceptable behavior. Lastly, and perhaps most importantly, it is the familial experience—sharing, conversing, and breaking bread (literally) with those in life who are most important to us. That is, after all, what good food and good drink are all about. In creating this dish, I tried to incorporate all those nostalgic tastes, smells, and experiences into a delicious finished product. I hope trying it conjures up similar feelings and memories for you. Cheers!

Serves eight to twelve

INGREDIENTS

- 1 ½ pounds mozzarella curd
- 1 tablespoon kosher salt
- 4 quarts water
- 2 sticks unsalted butter (plugra, if you can find it), cubed, brought to room temperature
- ⅓ cup garlic confit oil
- ½ cup garlic confit, recipe follows
- ½ cup finely grated parmesan reggiano
- ½ teaspoon tomato powder, recipe follows
- ½ teaspoon red pepper flakes, ground
- 2 teaspoons dried Sicilian oregano
- 1 teaspoon kosher salt (Diamond Crystal)
- 1 loaf rustic Italian bread
- ¼ cup minced fresh chives
- ½ cup chopped fresh Italian parsley
- ¼ cup rough-chopped fresh oregano leaves
- 1 cup heavy cream
- Good olive oil
- Maldon salt
- Tomato powder
- Fresh oregano leaves

EQUIPMENT

- Nonstick baking sheet or baking sheet with silpat liner
- Small sauce pan
- Pot that can hold 4 quarts+ of water
- Food processor
- 2 large metal mixing bowls
- Thermometer
- Wooden spoon
- Spice/coffee grinder

DIRECTIONS

1. Prepare the garlic confit and tomato powder a day in advance (see page 91).

2. While still cold, cut the mozzarella curd into ½-inch to ¾-inch cubes. Cutting the curd while still cold gives cleaner edges and makes for more efficient melting. Place the cut curds in a large mixing bowl and let come to room temperature. This will take about two to three hours.

3. Season the curds with the kosher salt and prepare a small mixing bowl of cold water next to the curds.

4. Preheat the oven to 450°F.

5. Bring 4 to 5 quarts of water up to a gentle simmer (170-180°F).

6. Add the butter, garlic confit, garlic oil, ¼ cup of the parmesan cheese, tomato powder, oregano, salt, and ground chili flakes to a food processor. Process until smooth, using a spatula to work in the bits on the side.

7. Cut the bread into extra thick slices (about ¾ inch to 1 inch). Then cut each slice in half. Liberally slather each side of the bread slices with the garlic confit butter and place on a baking sheet. Sprinkle each piece with a pinch of tomato powder and some of the remaining grated parmesan. Roast the bread until golden brown and lightly charred on the edges. Alternatively, you would not be gilding the lily if you grilled the bread over charcoal on both sides.

8. While the bread bakes, add the cream to a small sauce pan and bring to just under a simmer. You want the cream hot but not boiling.

9. Remove the bread from the oven. Mix the fresh chopped herbs together and sprinkle each piece with a few generous pinches of the herbs. Transfer the garnished slices of toast to a serving platter.

10. Once the cream is hot, distribute it evenly into three bowls and start the mozzarella-making process.

11. In the bowl of curds, pour hot water (180°F) around the edges of the bowl until it just covers the curds. Let the curds sit for about two minutes until they begin to soften and melt. Press the curds into the edge of the bowl with a wooden spoon or spatula and gently pack together. In another minute or two, they will form a mass. Once this happens, plunge your hands into the cold water and then grab one end of the mozzarella mass and pull from the hot water, slightly away from your body while guiding the remaining mass with your other hand. The mozzarella should stretch easily but in all likelihood will still be slightly lumpy.

12. Fold the stretched mass over itself once along its length and then once again to reform a more compact mass. Stretch the mass slowly again and fold over itself once more, then return to the water. Let sit for thirty seconds or so and cool your hands in the cold water bowl. Repeat the stretching process until no lumps remain and the curd is smooth and silky.

13. Once the curd is smooth and silky, assess the mass and get a sense of portion sizing. This recipe will make three large balls. Stretch the mass from the hot water and twist off a large chunk by tightly squeezing/pinching the curd below the desired portion with one hand and twisting the serving portion with your other hand. Return the remainder to the water. Take the twisted-off portion of mozzarella and fold the edges underneath. Pinch off to make a uniform ball/oval and immediately transfer to one of the serving bowls with the hot cream. Repeat the process to make the final two portions.

14. Garnish the cheese and cream with a couple glugs of good olive oil. Sprinkle generously with Maldon salt flakes, a pinch of tomato powder, and a few oregano leaves. Serve immediately with the garlic bread.

TOMATO POWDER INGREDIENTS

- 1 can whole plum tomatoes
  (I like San Marzano Brand)

TOMATO POWDER DIRECTIONS

1. Preheat the oven to 175°F or the nearest possible temperature with a rack positioned in the middle. Put the silpat liner in a four-sided sheet pan.

2. Drain the tomatoes and cut them in half crosswise. Add the halved tomatoes and their juices to a food processor, and process until smooth. Pour the tomato purée into a mesh strainer positioned over a bowl or pot in order to remove the seeds. Using a spoon or spatula, work the remaining tomato pulp and gel around the seeds through the strainer.

3. Spread the purée evenly over the surface of the silpat or non-stick sheet pan with a spatula. Dry the tomato purée in the oven, rotating the baking sheet every so often, until completely dehydrated and crisp, but not browned (about five to eight hours). Cool completely.

4. If your oven does not go as low as 175°F, or runs too hot, be sure to turn the oven on and off in forty-five-minute interval cycles until the tomatoes are completely dry.

5. Crumble the dried tomato into a spice/coffee grinder and grind to a fine powder.

6. Store indefinitely in an appropriately sized airtight container.

GARLIC CONFIT INGREDIENTS

- 1 cup peeled garlic cloves   • 2 cups olive oil

GARLIC CONFIT DIRECTIONS

1. Cut off and discard the root ends of the garlic cloves.

2. Put the cloves in a small saucepan, and add enough olive oil to cover them by about ½ to 1 inch—none of the garlic cloves should be poking through the oil.

3. Set the saucepan on the stove over low heat. The key to good garlic confit is to let it cook very gently.

4. Small bubbles will eventually come up through the oil, but the bubbles should not break the surface or roll aggressively.

5. If the oil starts to aggressively bubble, adjust the heat as necessary, and/or move the pan off the heat if it is cooking too quickly.

6. Return back to the burner after a few minutes of settling.

7. Cook the garlic for about forty minutes, stirring every five minutes or so, until the cloves are completely tender when pierced with the tip of a knife, but not browned.

8. Remove the saucepan from the heat and allow the garlic to cool in the oil.

9. Once cool, store in an airtight container in the refrigerator for up to a week.

Farhiya Isaac

 Farhiya Isaac was born in Somalia and lived there for eight years. Then, she moved to Uganda with her family and lived there for seven years. Finally, she arrived here in Ypsilanti with her family this past December, 2013. Farhiya loves to learn languages. She is fluent in Somali and Swahili. Her goal now is to learn English, and then Spanish. Farhiya's dream is to become a lawyer. A few things that she really enjoys are jogging, spending time with her parents, and listening to rap music.

AGE 16

How to Put on an Indian-Style Sari

The *Daqan Hindi labis* is a Somali-style clothing worn on the most special of days. It is to honor the president and the country. It has a specific way to be worn.

MATERIALS

- A long sari; must be red and white pattern
- A matching shirt

- Yellow *kull*, a specific necklace and armbands
- A short see-through head covering called a *shash*

- A yellow crown of beads

DIRECTIONS

1. Wrap the sari around your waist.

2. Wear the matching shirt over the sari.

3. Wear the *kull* over the shirt and on the arms.

4. Then you wear a short, matching *shash* that only covers the hair.

5. On top of the scarf, wear a yellow crown of beads that matches the *kull*.

My Book of Happiness

I AM SIXTEEN YEARS OLD. I was born in Somalia and lived in Uganda for eight years. I speak Somali and Swahili fluently.

I am really happy that I'm here now. I am extremely grateful that I now have the opportunity to go to school. Back in Uganda, I didn't have the chance to go to school, because I had to take care of my mother.

Now that I'm here, I have the chance to achieve my dream of becoming a lawyer or a government worker.

One memory that I will never forget is the time I went to the beach in Mombasa, Kenya. There, I swam in the ocean, ate really good fish, and spent time with family and friends. The fish I ate was so good. I've yet to taste anything as good as that fish.

Abdirahim Jeylani

Abdirahim Jeylani was born in Kenya, Africa, in 1998. His family is originally from Somalia. He speaks Somali and English. He and his family immigrated to the United States. He came to America in 2006 at the age of seven. He began attending Ypsilanti Community High School in 2013. He loves to play basketball and soccer and to communicate with people. Jeylani wants to be a world-famous basketball player.

AGE 15

How to Crossover in Basketball

The point of this move is to trick your defender. For the crossover to work, you have to master the way of dribbling the ball quickly, which is called ball handling. The offensive player uses the killer crossover to distract his defender. Michael Jordan used a killer crossover in the 1998 NBA Final Championship against the Utah Jazz, and he won his sixth championship.

Estimated time: Ten seconds

MATERIALS:

- Basketball
- Basketball shoes
- Shorts
- Fans
- Hoop
- Offender
- Defender
- Court

DIRECTIONS:

1. Dribble down the court and face your man.

2. Start at the free-throw line.

3. Look at your defender and look at where his legs are.

4. Then step up your speed.

5. Dribble the ball facing the right so the defender thinks that you're going to drive it into the hole.

6. Make sure that your shoulder, head, and your knees are facing the right side of the basket.

7. Act like you're going to the basket.

8. When you see your defender move, take advantage and dribble the ball to the left and drive the ball straight to the basket.

Jeylani's Exciting Time with His Family

I N 2010, MY FAMILY AND I WENT TO MINNEAPOLIS, Minnesota. We drove to the Somali Mall. When my mother, my brother Ahmed, and I got there, I saw many Somalis in the mall. I smelled *sobama* (a Somalian dish). I could hear adults and children talking and laughing.

"What are you looking at?" asked my mom.

"Noh-thing!" My mother is nice.

I saw a Somalian flag and I was proud of my country back home. I never saw more Somalis in a mall. I read a sign on a door that was written in Somali. My family and I ordered *sambusa*, *italwa*, *bariis*, and *baasta*. I tasted the spicy rice and juicy red tomato sauce. I could smell the lemon that was added to the *bariis*.

"Eat your food," said my mother to Ahmed. I was too hurried and ate a handful of rice, and I swallowed the whole thing so that my throat was full of rice. "Slow down, son, or you could be dead."

"Okay, Mom," I replied.

After lunch we went shopping for clothes. My lovely mom asked if I wanted to go with my aunt, and my aunt bought me Somali clothes. After we were done, we went to the Mall of America. Then I went home. As we were driving, I saw the lights in the buildings. I can hear people laughing. I can smell hamburger and *sambusi*.

Open Letter

Dear students of Ypsilanti Community High School,

What is education? Education is the knowledge, skill, and understanding that you get from attending a school, college, or university. Did you know that people in other countries don't have the chance to get an education?

Where can an education take you? Education can take you anywhere you want it to take you, whether you want to be a teacher, lawyer, NBA player, or the CEO of famous brand-name products. With a good education, you know how to help people and care for them. Without education, your chance of being successful in life is slim. With an education, you have a higher chance of being in a good position in life that is comfortable for you.

So do you want to be the person who is on the street and who has to sleep in the cold with a plastic bag for a blanket, or do you want to be the person who got their education and also graduated from college? He or she is the CEO of a brand-name product. This person probably is making $100,000-$2,000,000 and living a life of luxury with a Bugatti and mansion. Education is a tool that can take you far in life, and education is worth more than money.

So students, understand that education is a tool that you can use for all the problems you have in life. If you can use education as a tool, then nobody can take that from you. If you use education as a toy, then be ready for what life throws at you. I hope you use education as a tool and not as a toy.

Sincerely,

Jeylani

Efrain Herrera

 Efrain was born in Ypsilanti, Michigan. He speaks Spanish and English. His favorite foods are chicken and grilled cheese sandwiches. He enjoys reading a lot. He will be a paleontologist because he likes dinosaurs.

AGE 9

Pen-pal Letters

Dear pen-pal,

My name is Efrain. I speak English and Spanish. I am nine years old. My favorite book is *Angry Birds Star Wars: Lard Vader's Villains*. My teacher's name is Ms. Chenier. My favorite class is reading with the dogs. What is your name? How old are you? What's your favorite book? What language do you speak? What's your teacher's name?

Sincerely,

Efrain

Dear Efrain,

My name is Abdirahim Jeylani, but you can call me Jeylani. I'm fifteen years old. I'm from Somalia. Somalia is a country in Africa, and it's in the east side. So that means I speak Somalian. My favorite book is *100 Years of Hoops*. My teacher's name is Ms. Sirman. I have some questions for you. What is reading with the dogs? Do you like Adams? What is *Angry Birds Star Wars: Lard Vader's Villains*?

Sincerely,

Jeylani

....

Dear pen-pal Jeylani,

Angry Birds Star Wars: Lard Vader's Villains is about Lard Vader and his villains who want power, but they have to defeat the bird rebels, but the bird rebels were too brave and clever. I like the letter you gave me. I like Adams. I have some questions for you. What school are you in? Are you a boy or a girl? Is it fun there? Oh, one more thing, my Christmas tradition is that on Christmas Day we open presents. What is your holiday tradition?

Sincerely,

Efrain

Dear pen-pal Efrain,

I am a boy. I go to Ypsilanti Community High School. It's fun because of basketball. My Eid tradition is wearing nice clothes and spending good time with my family. Where are you from?

Sincerely,

Jeylani

....

Dear pen-pal Jeylani,

My parents are from Mexico, but I was born here in Ypsilanti. I often like cooking something. What food experience do you like? What kind of nice clothes do you wear? What do you do when you are spending time with your family? I cook hot dogs and sandwiches. My favorite sandwich is a chicken sandwich.

Sincerely,

Efrain

....

Dear pen-pal Efrain,

The experience I like is when the whole family is eating together. The kind of clothes I like is sportswear. When I'm spending time with my family, I like to play sports. What type of shows do you like to watch?

Sincerely,

Jeylani

Dear pen-pal Jeylani,

I like watching *The Pirates Who Don't Do Anything*. It's about three cabin boys who work in a restaurant. My class is learning about Martin Luther King Jr. Adams feels like a family because my class feels great. How is your school like a family? Oh, one more thing, we have lots of work to do every day at home.

Sincerely,

Efrain

⋯⋯⋯⋯⋯⋯⋯⋯⋯⋯⋯⋯⋯⋯⋯⋯⋯⋯⋯⋯⋯⋯⋯⋯

Dear pen-pal Efrain,

In my health class, we talk about how to be healthy. The way my class is like a family is that the class is not mean, and they don't say something bad about you. Also they like to share snacks. Are the kids in your class mean to you? Do they share snacks with you?

Sincerely,

Jeylani

⋯⋯⋯⋯⋯⋯⋯⋯⋯⋯⋯⋯⋯⋯⋯⋯⋯⋯⋯⋯⋯⋯⋯⋯

Dear pen-pal Jeylani,

I am sick from talking, all the snow days, and I can't think. Most often, I like watching TV.

Sincerly,

Efrain

MIYOKO HONMA

PRESENTS

NO-BAKE
YOGURT CAKE

Miyoko Honma is the owner of Café Japon and L'Esprit de Miyoko. She is a *boulangere* and *patissiere* who is deploying an authentic, online French bakery/boutique. She will be offering various croissants, cakes, macarons, and confitures using local ingredients. Currently, she is further developing her knowledge and skills for this phase of business.

This recipe is simple and is prepared quickly, but is very tasty, especially if you use organic yogurt (not necessarily Greek), heavy whipping cream, and milk. These organic ingredients are easy to find in local grocery stores. Hopefully this will allow many people to try this recipe.

INGREDIENTS

- About 3 ounces of cookies such as vanilla wafers
- 3 tablespoons butter (soft)
- 1 ½ cups milk (½ cup set aside for gelatin)

- 1 cup sugar
- 3 envelopes gelatin (mix with ½ cup of milk, set aside)
- 2 ½ cups plain yogurt
- 2 cups heavy whipping cream

- Juice from ½ of a lemon
- 1 teaspoon vanilla extract or essence

DIRECTIONS

1. Roll out cookies in a plastic bag to make crumbs.
2. Mix the crumbs with softened butter.
3. Put the mixture on the bottom of a spring-form pan and put it in a refrigerator.
4. Mix gelatin with ½ cup of milk.
5. Put milk and sugar in a pot and bring to a simmer. Remove the pot from the heat and add the gelatin/milk mixture.
6. Add the yogurt, heavy whipping cream, vanilla extract/essence, and lemon juice to the milk mixture. Mix well.
7. Put the contents into the spring-form pan and let it set.
8. Serve with fruits or fruit sauce.

Karam Kadhum

 Karam M. Kadhum was born in 1996 on August 24. He likes playing soccer, swimming, and eating Arabic food. He is from Iraq; he lived in Baghdad with his family. He has five brothers. He is the youngest. He would like to finish school and go to college. He would like to be an engineer or a doctor.

AGE 17

Recipe for Falafel and Hummus

I think these are great foods because they have a special taste. Once you have tasted these, you will want more! These are Arabic foods from the Middle East.

HUMMUS INGREDIENTS

- 1 cup chickpeas
- ½ cup olive oil
- 2 tablespoons tahini

HUMMUS DIRECTIONS

Put all ingredients in a blender and spin for one-and-a-half minutes, or until uniform. Serve with slices of lemon, tomatoes, and parsley in the middle to make it look beautiful and delicious! Scoop up the hummus with pita or Lebanese bread.

This will take about thirty minutes to prepare.

FALAFEL INGREDIENTS

- 2 cups chickpeas
- 2 tablespoons salt
- Sunflower oil for frying

FALAFEL DIRECTIONS

Place the chickpeas and salt into a small grinder and grind until crunchy. Form into falafel balls. Take the falafel balls and place them in a frying pan with sunflower oil. Fry until crisp. Eat while hot or place in Iraqi bread with fresh tomatoes, pickles, and lettuce. Spread special Iraqi sauce and enjoy!

My Two Beautiful Weekends

MY MOM AND DAD, MY TWO BROTHERS Ali and Ahmed, and I went to Irbil, a beautiful state in Iraq. We saw the beautiful Furat River and went to the mountains in the north. We woke up at 9AM and left at 10AM. We walked through and packed a lunch and a hookah. You can see everything when you are on the mountains. I really liked it; we stayed in Irbil ten days, and I went with my two oldest brothers to go swim in the river. My favorite part of the trip was swimming in the river because it was hot and the water was cold and clear, like the sea. But it tasted sweet. You can drink from it. If you put an apple in the water from the mountains, it will split because it is so cold. Only my brothers and I swam. After our vacation, we went back to Baghdad, to our home.

Another time, my grandfather called my mom, and he said, "I want to take Karam to the river." I felt happy and went to take a shower, and we left at 12PM. The river in Baghdad is named Dijla. I felt happy because my grandfather was with me and we were fishing. He told me about his past, when he was my age. He told me about when he was a boy, he told me about his good father, and told me about his school. He said he loved school and the teachers loved him. The river looked like blue. And he told me he loved songs and that when he was a boy, he was a singer.

People in Iraq go to the river once a month when it is nice outside. We go because you can watch TV any day, but when we go to the river, we can eat lunch outside, sit down in the garden when the weather is good, and play soccer together.

Open Letter

My dear friend,

You are a new student, and I want to give you advice about this school. In this school, some people want to fight, but I want to help you make friends. I want to get to know you, and I know a lot about this school.

Be a good student, study together with people, don't fight, sit with new students at lunch to make friends. Be kind to other students. The lunch in this school is good, especially the BBQ chicken! I hope this advice helps you to be a good student.

Sincerely,

Karam

Mohamed Ali Doumbouya

Mohamed Ali was born in Ypsilanti, Michigan. He enjoys playing video games and playing with computers. He wants to be a basketball player! His languages are Mandingo and English. His favorite foods are hot wings, hot dogs, and hot soup! His favorite sport is martial arts.

AGE 8

How to Eat Dinner

INGREDIENTS

- Remote control
- TV
- Couch
- Rice
- Peanut butter sauce

DIRECTIONS

I get the remote. Then I turn the TV on. I sit on the couch. I turn on Netflix and find *Johnny Test*. I watch it, and I wait until my mother calls me to go eat dinner. I eat rice with peanut butter sauce. When I am done, I wash my dishes. Then I watch TV again.

Pen-pal Letters

Dear pen-pal,

My name is Mohamed. I speak Mandingo and English. My age is seven. My favorite book is *Diary of a Wimpy Kid*. I am in second grade. My favorite sport is basketball. My height is 3.8 feet. My favorite teacher is Ms. V. My favorite candies are Butterfinger and Jolly Ranchers. My favorite team is the Miami Heat. My favorite pet is a dog. Where do you live? Are you going to send me money, please? I want to know your name. You guys are the best. What is your school's name? My school's name is Adams Academy. You guys are the best high schoolers. Can you guys come and visit us? Please, you guys are the best!

Sincerely,

Mohamed Ali

Hi Mohamed Ali,

My name is Karam. I speak Arabic and English. My age is seventeen. My favorite sport is soccer. I like to play on the computer, looking with my friend and seeing the news for my country, Iraq. I came from Iraq two months ago. And I miss my family. They live in Baghdad, Iraq. It's a big city, and it's so nice. I want to ask you, do you live here in Ypsilanti? How long have you been here in the USA? I like to watch movies, sports, and news, and I like swimming. Do you have brothers or sisters? Do you like any games? I have five brothers, and I don't have any sisters. I live here with my brother. Thank you for writing me.

From,

Karam

....

Dear Karam,

I do have a brother and a sister. You have a lot of brothers! Do you like to play sports? Well, I like playing! Do you want to be my friend? I would like to meet you. What grade are you in? I am in second grade. I speak English and Mandingo! I was born in Michigan! I like to play video games. My favorite video game is *Call of Duty*. What is your favorite video game? My family lives in Guinea. I love Guinea! What kind of songs do you like? My favorite song is "What Does the Fox Say?" I am a friendly friend. My favorite holiday is Christmas. My last name is very hard to say. My name is Mohamed Ali Doumbouya. What is your last name? On Christmas, my family gives me presents.

From,

Mohamed Ali

Hi Mohamed,

Yes, I like sports. I like playing soccer and swimming. Sure, we can be friends. I would like to meet you, too. I speak a little English, and I speak Arabic. I was born in my country, Iraq, in Baghdad. My favorite video game is *FIFA*. It's a soccer game. My family lives in Baghdad. Now I live with my big brother, and my family lives in Iraq. My favorite music is hip-hop. My favorite holiday is Christmas because I like snow. It is not hard. My name is Karam Mohamed Kadhum. What do you like about Christmas?

From,

Karam

Dear Karam,

I do like Christmas. I would like to meet your family! I am from Michigan. My family is from Africa. My favorite music is rap and hip-hop. Do you like to play in the snow? Well, I like to play in the snow. I like to make an igloo. My family makes rice and chicken for dinner. Oh, and sauce. My favorite part of the day is in the afternoon. My favorite month is December because it is going to be Christmas. Santa is coming to town.

From,

Mohamed Ali

Dear Karam,

It's so cold. Do you like to play in the snow? I do a little bit but sometimes I don't. I play on the computer when I don't. I bet you were sick. I was sick yesterday. People are not going to school! What kind of school do you go to? I go to Adams Academy! My mom and my dad are from Africa! I know a lot of things in Africa because I went there! Do you like to shop and read? I like my school because you can learn and read and do math and play with materials. My favorite sports at my school and the whole state and city are karate and basketball. Do you celebrate Dr. Martin Luther King Jr. Day? Well, I do. Do you like to go to places and play? Well, I do, too. Goodbye.

Sincerely,

Mohamed

P.S. How is your school family-like? Mine is a family because we have a lot of people and we are friends, that's why we are a family. Bye!!!

....

Dear Mohamed,

I like snow and to play in the snow. But I don't like cold. Me too, I play on the laptop when we have a lot of snow. And me too, I was sick. I go to Ypsilanti Community High School. I'm from Iraq. I have been here just three months. And I don't like reading. I like shopping. Me too, I like my school because I don't like to sit at home. My school is like a family with my friends, and I don't have a lot of friends because I'm new in the USA. Do you like to drive? And do you like boats? Do you like swimming?

Karam

....

Dear Karam,

I don't like to play in the snow too, just a little bit. I fight a little bit with my brother. Is your school boring? Well, my school is not. My school is cool. Is your school cool? Do you like to play video games? I do. Do you play *Grand Theft Auto*? Well, I do. I like to write with you. Tell me your favorite stuff. Okay. Bye.

Sincerely,

Mohamed

SAVA LELCAJ

PRESENTS

PINK GREEK DRESSING

Sava Lelcaj is the owner of three food venues in Ann Arbor: Sava's Restaurant; Babo, a fresh food market; and a new tapas bar, Aventura. Since opening Sava's State Street Cafe in 2007, her unique blend of passion and business savvy has brought her community of restaurants the kind of success that is hard to find and keep in the competitive downtown market. Sava remains committed to bringing unique, high quality culinary experiences to Ann Arbor.

When I was in high school, I was lucky enough to work at a fabulous Greek restaurant that served the BEST Greek dressing on Earth! Famous for this amazing dressing, they served every meal with fresh bread and a salad topped with their famous dressing. Not only did it taste amazing, it was, get this . . . PINK! I loved this restaurant and loved this dressing.

Years later, when I was developing the menu for my own restaurant in Hazel Park, I decided to come up with my own powder-pink Greek dressing. Not having the base knowledge for such a dressing, I went through about one hundred different ingredients and almost as many combinations before finally perfecting the perfect dressing in the perfect shade of pink. I discovered the amazing properties of beet powder! It provided that extra special note to my dressing and provided the powder-pink hue. This same dressing made my Ann Arbor restaurant Sava's State Street Cafe famous. My chefs at Sava's make it today with the same TLC that I did and serve it with the same amount of pride that I did so many years back. We also utilize beet powder in many of our other recipes at all of my restaurants. It makes the food so tasty and adds that strong, dominant hue of PINK to my food!

Go, go beet powder and go, go GIRL POWER!

INGREDIENTS

- 2 cups mayonnaise
- ½ cup water
- 2 tablespoons extra virgin olive oil
- 3 tablespoons red wine vinegar
- ½ tablespoon sugar

- ½ tablespoon beet powder (heaping)
- ½ tablespoon each of onion powder, dried thyme, dried parsley, dried celery salt (or two tablespoons dry Italian dressing seasoning)

- ¾ tablespoon oregano
- ¾ tablespoon garlic powder
- ½ teaspoon salt
- ¼ teaspoon black pepper

DIRECTIONS

1. Combine all ingredients except oil and water in large bowl.
2. Blend all ingredients with an immersion blender or hand mixer.
3. Slowly drizzle in oil while continuing to mix.
4. Add water to adjust consistency.
5. Serve chilled over your favorite greens!

Dulcinée Landa

 Dulcinée was born on October 6, 1997. She has lived in Ypsilanti, Michigan, for four months. She was born in Kinshasa, the capital of the Democratic Republic of Congo. She used to go to Lincoln High School but now goes to YCHS. Dulcinée loves chocolate but does not really like American food. When she has free time, Dulcinée likes to read books. She loves rap, dancing, and drawing. She has many friends who always help her when she does not understand things, especially her best friend, Aaron Cofield, whom she loves. She would like to be a lawyer and have a family with two children.

AGE 16

Recipe for Scrambled Eggs

Total preparation: Fifteen minutes

INGREDIENTS

- 2 eggs
- 5 potatoes
- 1 tablespoon oil
- 1 teaspoon sugar
- Ketchup to taste

DIRECTIONS

1. Break eggs in a bowl.
2. Add sugar.
3. Mix eggs and sugar.
4. Peel and cut potatoes.
5. Oil pan, and add eggs and potatoes.
6. Cook for five minutes.
7. Put on a plate and add ketchup.

Learning English

WHEN I CAME TO SCHOOL FOR MY FIRST DAY at Lincoln when I was sixteen, I received more stuff, notebooks, pencils, etc. After that, my principal showed me the hallway. Then, after my first class, I was lost and I didn't know how to get to my second class, so I was still there until the time came for me to go to the next class. It was very difficult for me. When I was going to my third class, my teacher asked me, "Why were you not in your second class?" and it was very difficult to explain why.

When I arrived at my first day of school, it was boring because I couldn't understand many things. For example, when I went to take my lunch, I saw a girl, and she said to me, "You're a pretty girl," and I said, "No," because I couldn't understand English. When I got to my house, I told my cousin there was a person who said to me "you're pretty" and I said "no." After, my cousin teased me and said, "You're stupid!" My cousin told me to go back tomorrow and then say to her, "Thank you," and, "I am pretty. You're very pretty, also."

The next day I told her what my cousin said, and she said, "I understand that you don't know how to speak English." She seemed mean, and I didn't like her.

Now, I can speak and understand English much better. I learned that it's hard to learn a language that you do not know and be in an environment where everyone speaks a language you do not know. I'm glad because a person can understand what I'm saying, and I hope that I am able to learn faster what remains.

BEN NEWMAN

PRESENTS

HOMEMADE BAGELS

Ben Newman is co-founder of the Detroit
Institute of Bagels, an eatery serving fine bagels
for the masses in a century-old building in the
Corktown neighborhood of Detroit. Ben, who holds
a Master of Urban Planning from the University of
Michigan, started the bagel business in 2010 out
of his apartment. Soon after the Detroit Institute
of Bagels opened its doors in 2013, the company
received a $50,000 grant from the Old Tiger
Stadium Conservancy Fund, awarded on-site by
Senator Carl Levin, to help cover the costs of the
building renovation.

This is the recipe we used when we started making bagels out of our flat in Cork-town. While we've gotten close to replicating these bagels on a larger scale at the store, there is something about this recipe and the labor involved that makes the resulting product so enjoyable. So enjoy!

Makes about eighteen bagels

SPONGE

1. Find a BIG bowl and spatula.

2. Mix 600 grams (4 cups) of high-gluten flour and 2.5 grams (about ¾ teaspoon) of instant yeast.

3. Add 575 grams (just a touch under 2 ½ cups) of water.

4. Let rise for about two hours until sponge starts to form bubbles and about doubles in size.

DOUGH

1. Add 1.5 grams (½ teaspoon) of yeast to sponge, and mix.

2. Add 20 grams (2 tablespoons) of barley malt syrup, and mix.

3. Add 14 grams of salt (1 ½ tablespoons), and mix again.

4. Add 525 grams (3 ½ cups) of flour and knead until dough has a polished finish.

5. Divide dough into 100 gram balls, let sit for ten minutes, and form into bagel shape. Let bagels rest for about twenty more minutes and put in refrigerator overnight.

NEXT DAY

1. Preheat oven to 500°F.

2. Bring 6kg (about 6 quarts) of water to a boil.

3. Boil four to six bagels (however many will fit in your pot) for one minute per side, top with desired toppings, and bake for eighteen minutes. Flip bagels and finish baking for two to three minutes.

Guy Landa

Guy Landa was born October 16, 1998, in Kinshasa, Democratic Republic of Congo. He went to Lincoln High School and now goes to YCHS. Guy loves animals, especially dogs. He enjoys soccer. He would like to be a veterinarian.

AGE 16

Recipe for White Beans

Estimated time: One-and-a-half hours

INGREDIENTS

- 2 cups white beans
- 1 tomato
- 1 onion
- 1 clove garlic

DIRECTIONS

Boil beans for one hour. Dice tomatoes, onions, and garlic. Add vegetables to cooked beans and cook a while longer.

Mon Voyage aux États-Unis
(My Trip to the United States)

JE ME SUIS RÉVEILLÉ LE MATIN *pour partir à l'aéroport de Kinshasa pour le voyage. J'ai joué aux jeux de Zuma. Après que l'avion est arrivé a 22h00 nous avons fait une transite á Paris. Dans l'avion de Delta pour Detroit, j'ai vomi parce que je ne me sentais pas bien.*

J'ai fait le voyage au US parce que j'avais envie de continuer mes études universitaires pour devenir médecin vétérinaire car cela me plait et je pense que dès que je finirai high school j'irai à l'université.

J'aimerais être médecin vétérinaire parce que j'aime beaucoup les animaux. Quand j'étais au Congo, j'avais un petit chien au nom de "Windyski" et je l'aime beaucoup. Quand je voyais mon papa vacciner les chiens ou les chats comme j'ai toujours envie de faire et je trouve que la seule façon d'imiter mon papa c'est devenir médecin vétérinaire comme lui.

I WOKE UP IN THE MORNING to leave for the Kinshasa Airport for the trip. I played a game called "Zuma" on the way. After the plane arrived at 10:00PM, we passed through Paris. On our way to Detroit, I threw up on the plane because I didn't feel well.

I came to the United States because I want to continue my education at a university so that I can become a veterinarian because I enjoy that, and I think that when I finish high school I will go to university.

I would like to be a veterinarian because I really like animals. When I was in the Democratic Republic of Congo, I had a small dog named Windyski, and I loved him. When I saw my dad vaccinating dogs or cats, I always wanted to do that and I think that the only way to be like my dad is to become a veterinarian like him.

SYLVIA NOLASCO-RIVERS

PRESENTS

PILAR'S CHEESE AND LOROCO PUPUSAS AND CURTIDO

Sylvia Nolasco-Rivers is the owner and founder of Pilar's Tamales, an Ann Arbor restaurant specializing in Salvadoran food. Pilar's, which opened in 2000, is celebrating its fourteenth year of providing the Ann Arbor community incredible tamales, pupusas, and more. Sylvia is dedicated to building community and believes that everything that is good is worth sharing.

Pupusas are a very special part of Salvadoran culture and heritage and are recognized throughout Central America as a food originating in El Salvador. Pupusas are street food and can be eaten for breakfast, lunch, and dinner. You cannot have a pupusa without curtido, and you cannot have curtido without a pupusa.

In Ann Arbor, I am often called the tamale lady. There are labels like this in El Salvador, too: there's the tortilla lady, the pupusa lady. When I was a little girl growing up in El Salvador, if my mom was too busy to cook dinner, she would say to me, "Can you go down to the corner and get some pupusas from the pupusa lady?" I have such gratitude toward these women; they are amazing. They make their pupusas on a *comal*, which is a ceramic grill that sits right over a fire. Loroco, a Salvadoran flower, is a traditional filling. The flowers look like the tip of an asparagus stalk. People go crazy for Loroco pupusas here at Pilar's, but, if you can't find Loroco, you can easily substitute poblano, jalapeño, or even bell peppers.

PUPUSAS: MASA MIX INGREDIENTS

- 4 cups Maseca corn flour
- 3 ½ cups cold water

PUPUSAS: MASA MIX DIRECTIONS

1. Add water to flour in mixing bowl. With either a mixer or by hand, blend mix to an even consistency. Mix for no more than five minutes.

2. Store in bowl covered with damp cloth.

3. Set aside and prepare filling.

FILLING MIX INGREDIENTS

- 3 ½ cups Mexican cheese blend
- 1 ½ cups pickled Loroco flowers—if you cannot find Loroco flowers, feel free to substitute poblano, jalapeño, or even bell peppers
- ½ teaspoon salt (or to taste)

FILLING MIX DIRECTIONS

1. Strain Loroco in a strainer, and finely chop up by hand or in a food processor.

2. Mix cheese and Loroco together, and evenly blend by hand.

3. Set aside in a bowl covered with a damp cloth.

PUPUSAS DIRECTIONS

1. Heat the grill to 350°F or heat a skillet to medium heat.

2. Have ready a small bowl of water or a kitchen cooking water sprayer.

3. Shape 2 ½ ounces (about ⅓ of a cup) of the masa mix into a round the size of a golf ball. (You don't need to add the dimples.) Press out the ball into a four-inch patty shape.

4. Scoop out 1 ½ ounces (about 3 tablespoons) of the cheese mix and put in the center of the masa round. Close pupusa around the cheese, and reshape into a ball.

5. Pupusas are now ready to grill.

6. On a pre-heated dry grill (DO NOT OIL), throw on your pupusas and lightly spritz with water to prevent them from drying out.

7. Cook undisturbed for four minutes, then flip over and spritz again. Cook on second side for four minutes.

8. Flip again, and cook on each side for two minutes following the same procedure.

9. When your pupusa puffs up, it is ready to eat! Enjoy with curtido.

CURTIDO INGREDIENTS

- 1 head cabbage, julienne cut
- 1 Spanish onion, julienne cut
- 1 ½ pounds carrots, peeled and cut into thin rounds
- 2 tablespoons dry oregano
- 1 ½ teaspoons salt
- 1 ½ cups apple cider vinegar

CURTIDO DIRECTIONS

1. Combine all ingredients in a large bowl and mix thoroughly by hand.

Miguel Leon-Jimenez

 Miguel Leon-Jimenez was born on July 24, 1995. He was raised in one of the biggest cities in the world, Mexico City, where most of his life was constrained by difficult situations. He left his country to get a better education. He loves to write, think, and philosophize. His dream is to be remembered as a man of Hispanic pride.

AGE 18

How to Be Successful in Life

Life is about trying, making mistakes, and learning, led by focusing. The more you focus on what you have to do, the more successful you'll be. In life you'll meet a lot of people. People who will be there for you when you need them, even people who will want to see you fail. Ignore those who want to keep you down, because you aren't getting anything by listening to them. Rather than losing your time on them, focus on what you have to do, because time is valuable. Living life the way you want it to be, not how others want to see you, is the key to being successful. Just like you never stop learning, you never stop achieving goals. There is not a limit in life.

Donde Muere El Sol

"T HERE! WHERE THE SUN DIES." Those are the words that my uncle would say to me every time he would leave the house for days and I would ask him, "Where are you going?" I was probably twelve years old, and I didn't understand what he was trying to say by that. Now that I've grown up, I can see the other side of his guitar and realize what he was going through—things that no one could understand but him, and his problems. Waking up in the morning from the beautiful sound of his guitar and singing is the best memory I have of him.

My uncle is special to me. Most of my childhood I was raised with him, my uncle Miguel, and my brothers. At some point while I was in elementary school, he left to go to the United States for a better education. Once he tried college, he chose his passion for the guitar over a pencil. His name was Ivan. His appearance was unique. He would always wear ripped jeans, old shoes where you could see his socks showing because they were tattered, and a dirty looking sweater.

Last time I saw him was a sunny Saturday in 2008. It was probably 7:00AM when my mom woke me up. *"Miguel, levantate y alistate que van a llevar a tu tio al aeropuerto."* She told me to get ready because we were taking my uncle to the airport. I knew that was the last time I was going to see him. As we were on our way to the airport, he was telling me and my brother to listen to my mom on everything she said and to take care of her. I wanted to cry, but I didn't.

Next thing I knew, we were walking into the airport as he was playing the guitar while having a conversation with us. Waiting at the gate and seeing airplanes pass by was bittersweet. We were enjoying our last moment together, yet I wanted to cry because I knew that in a few minutes he was going to be in one of those planes but I held my tears. Suddenly the gate attendant called his flight to Mexico. We stood up, and, as I was talking to my brother, both of my uncles were talking. I got distracted for a minute, and, when I turned to where he was standing. I saw him walking away with his guitar in his hand. I was hoping to hear a goodbye from him, but he just walked away. I couldn't hold my tears, and I started crying. He turned around to wave at us. I could tell that my tears broke his resolve, so he stepped out of the line and quickly walked back toward me. He handed me his guitar without saying anything, hugged me, and walked back to the line. Once I had his guitar, for some reason, I stopped crying. I guess that was his way to say goodbye. I didn't have to ask where he was going. I knew exactly. He was going where the sun dies.

Open Letter

Dear YCHS students,

As a senior of YCHS, I have a different point of view from you all. I have noticed good things and bad things that are happening in YCHS. One of the main problems in this high school is the respect between teachers and students. For what I've noticed, there seems to be an attitude with some students. Students come to school unprepared and act like they can just sit and not follow instructions, making the whole class stop. These actions take students' time away from learning. The fact that the high school cafeteria does not have a variety of food makes them complain about it, even though they eat it. Students are bored of receiving the same meals every other day. Finally, the school library does not have enough books, and there isn't anyone running it.

These issues are important because I care about the high school community. I've been coming to this high school since my freshman year. Because I have enough experience in this high school, I think I'm the best person to give this advice.

As a student in YCHS, I've seen there is not an equality with many students. Some security guards seem to get along better with some students, so that when they see them walking around the school, they don't get their attention. YCHS needs individual and equal treatment. The school gives the exact same meal every other day. A lot of students have complained about the food. To solve this problem, I think changing the meal every day could make a big difference. It would also be helpful if students volunteered to organize books in the library.

YCHS has great teachers who actually care about the students. They make sure they get the concept, enough help, and different resources to get help at home. Good examples are Ms. Heath, Ms. Sirman, Ms. Tiernan, and Mr. Oldford. I hope YCHS continues to improve. YCHS is a great school.

Sincerely,

Miguel Leon-Jimenez

Kaleb Dawit

 Kaleb Dawit was born in Ethiopia. He enjoys playing video games. He speaks English and Amharic. His favorite foods are pizza and chicken breast. He wants to be an astronomer when he grows up. His favorite book is *The Yearling*. His favorite TV shows are *The Simpsons*, *American Dad*, *Family Guy*, *The Cleveland Show*, and *The Big Bang Theory*.

AGE 12

Recipe for Cheese Pizza with Pepperoni and Hot Sauce

Today I will show you how to make cheese pizza. So first I will introduce myself. My name is Kaleb.

INGREDIENTS

- Crust
- Cheese
- Hot sauce
- Pepperoni
- Tomato sauce

DIRECTIONS

1. First you buy the crust and put the crust on the table.

2. Put the cheese on the crust and put the pepperoni on the crust and put the tomato sauce on the crust and put it in the oven. When it is ready, you eat it with hot sauce.

Pen-pal Letters

Dear pen-pal,

I eat my traditional food like pasta with sauce, beef, and rice. I like to cook pizza. We don't really go out, but sometimes we do. Some questions for you: What are you doing for your New Year's resolution? List things that you celebrate. What's your favorite TV show? Do you like math and science? What's your favorite book?

Sincerely,

Kaleb

Dear pen-pal,

It is nice to hear from you. What's your favorite pizza? I've been working after school. I work as a waiter at Los Amigos, a Mexican restaurant. For New Year's, I went to a party with friends and enjoyed the night. I celebrate Christmas, New Year's, and Cinco de Mayo. My favorite TV show is *LA Ink*. It is a tattoo show. I do like math, however, I'm not as good as I wish I could be. And I don't like science. I don't have a favorite book because I don't like reading.

Sincerely,

Miguel

....

Dear Miguel,

I am happy to get your letter back. My favorite pizza is cheese pizza. I like my school and the teachers. I wish there were lots more students in the school, and I wish they were smart because the school would improve like a family. In our school, there is an area you can make friends and make things called engineering. In engineering, you can do whatever you want in a fun place. My school is like a family because I was talking with my friends and playing with my friends. And I am enjoying playing and talking with my friends.

Sincerely,

Kaleb

Dear Kaleb,

Nice! I can tell you're happy. Tell me more about the place to make friends. This weekend was okay. I worked, like always. I met new people to chill with at work. I am going to a party on Friday, and I'm expecting to have fun. Who is your favorite teacher? Who do you hang out with the most at school? I am really happy that University of Michigan won against Eastern.

Sincerely,

Miguel

....

Dear Miguel,

How are you? I am okay. My favorite teacher is Mr. Moore, and I hang out with nobody. I had a great weekend, and I was watching TV. I met a guy named Losany and his nickname is "Yo-yo." He is a great friend. My favorite video games are *Grand Theft Auto 5* and *Need for Speed: Most Wanted*. What's your friend's name? What's your favorite video game? What's your favorite teacher?

Sincerely,

Kaleb

JOEL PANOZZO

JOEL PANOZZO

THE LUNCH ROOM'S SOUTH-WEST SALAD DRESSING

Joel Panozzo and his business partner Phillis Englebert are the owners and founders of The Lunch Room. The Lunch Room, which began as a pop-up venture and then a food cart, is now a fully-established restaurant serving high-quality vegan food out of Ann Arbor's Kerrytown neighborhood. Joel and Phillis are committed to pursuing their values through their work, including freedom, creativity, fun, egalitarianism, social justice, and community.

When we started this project over three years ago, I would have never imagined myself at the Farmer's Market years later, buying hundreds of pounds of cabbage at a time. Our restaurant is only a few steps from the market. It has allowed me to be involved in this magical process of chatting with the farmers about their week's harvest and serving that same cabbage in this salad moments later. Food has the power to bring folks together like no other medium. What started as small pop-up dinners serving our friends on cafeteria trays grew into what it is now because of the community that surrounded the food.

INGREDIENTS

- 2 cups Vegenaise or any other mayonnaise
- 2 whole chiles, plus 2 table-spoons of the sauce from a can of chipotle chiles in adobo sauce (Substitutions for this ingredient are not recommended. Use more or less sauce/chiles to adjust for desired spiciness.)
- 1 teaspoon ground cumin
- 1 teaspoon granulated garlic
- ¼ teaspoon oregano
- 1 teaspoon sea salt
- ¼ cup of chopped cilantro leaves
- 2 tablespoons of fresh-squeezed lime juice

DIRECTIONS

1. Place all of the ingredients in a food processor, and blend until the ingredients are incorporated and the chiles have broken down.

2. This dressing works great on other salads or as a dip. Try your own Southwest Salad. Start with a bed of green and/or red shredded cabbage, with a hearty scoop of brown rice and black beans. Sliced avocados and fresh salsa brighten the dish, and some tortilla chips give an extra crunch.

Isai Leon-Valenzuela

Isai was born in Veracruz, Mexico, on February 22, 1997, and, when he was three years old, his mom moved to the United States. He stayed in Mexico with his grandparents. When he was four years old, he went to school and had really bad grades. When Isai was in fifth grade, his mom moved to Mexico with the family. Then she went back to the United States, and he moved with her. On his first day in the USA, he felt nervous and excited, and two months later, in 2008, he started school and learned some English. At the age of fifteen, he started to work and he didn't want to go to school anymore, because school was hard. Three months later, he returned to school. Isai started to drive, and now he is still going to school. He likes to eat Greek food and play soccer. Isai enjoys riding his bicycle. Isai hopes to get better at school.

AGE 17

Recipe for *Chilaquiles*

Co-written by Sheridan Zaldivar and Isai Leon-Valenzuela

You should eat *chilaquiles* because it is better than American food and better than Taco Bell. Taco Bell is a really fake food. The *chilaquiles* have a very good taste.

Estimated time: Twenty to thirty minutes

INGREDIENTS

- *Queso fresco* (whole milk cheese)
- *Crema* (cream)
- *Tortillas de maíz* (corn tortilla chips, any type will work)
- *Aceite de maíz* (corn oil)
- *Lechuga* (lettuce)

- *Chiles verdes* (green chiles)
- *Tomatillos* (green tomatoes)
- *Cebolla* (white onion)
- *Huevos* (scrambled eggs)
- Skillet
- *Cuchara* (spoon) to stir/mix
- Small plate

- Fork *para comer* (to eat)
- *Un refresco de Coca-Cola o Sangria* (a beverage like Coca-Cola or Sangria, which is a type of soda)
- *Napkin para que limpiar tus manos y boca . . . quizás* (napkin to clean your hands and mouth . . . maybe)

DIRECTIONS

1. *Primero*, make the salsa: green tomatoes, onion, water, *chiles verdes*, garlic, salt—put everything in a blender until it is very smooth, then put it on the stove in a pan to heat it up.

2. *Poner las tortilla chips en el pan o ponerle lechuga, queso, crema y despues servir en un plato y comes. Tomar Sangria o el refresco en un vaso, también.* (Put the tortilla chips in the pan and add the lettuce, cheese, and cream, and after serve on a plate and eat. Pour the Sangria or drink in a glass, too.)

Everything was Different

WOW! LOOK AT ALL THE FREEWAYS AND CARS! I was thinking. We were waiting in Houston for my mom's boyfriend to get to Houston from Michigan. It was my first time in the United States. I didn't speak any English, and I was excited to get to Michigan.

Everything was different in Michigan. First, there seemed to be more organization with traffic and even more police. Then, I got into the apartment and everything looked different. I have never lived in an apartment, only houses. Finally, I couldn't understand any words in English, so I stayed quiet, but I stay quiet a lot.

I am from Mexico

I am from Mexico

I see the same dusty roads I use to travel anywhere

I feel the hot sun as it bakes my skin

I hear the rooster as he crows to wake me up each morning

I taste the tamales my grandma made with her hands

I smell the coffee my grandma drank every morning

Bryan Lopez

 Bryan is a junior at Ypsilanti Community High School and was born on May 8, 1996. He is from El Salvador. He enjoys soccer, and his favorite team is F.C. Barcelona. He loves to travel to New York. He loves his family in New York and the ambiance of the city; also, the delis there are very good. Bryan loves to drive a stick shift. He enjoys learning about the features in other cars, mostly how they function. Bryan hopes to go to college and make something of himself. He wants to be able to support his parents in the near future, without them having to worry about going to work.

AGE 17

How to be in a Rock Band

If you want the eighties to thrive once again and in your heart, join a band that will revive the past!

The amount of time it will take to finish these steps will depend on the person or the amount of effort put into the band to be impressive.

THINGS YOU NEED

- Instruments (a lot of them)
- Subwoofer (enhance sound)
- Microphones
- Rebellious attitude
- Piercings
- Tattoos

DIRECTIONS

1. Pick your rebellious attitude, whether you want to be goth or street rebel, be the influence to the crowd; do things like wreck guitars.

2. Pick a genre, whether punk rock or heavy metal, or even eighties rock. Find three to four other members.

3. Find your certain instrument, like a bass guitar. There are different styles of guitars, so pick a certain style and stick with it.

4. Practice the type of music you want the public to hear, most importantly the singing. Practice makes perfect—you need to practice so at an important gig you don't mess up.

5. Put your band out there. For example, post fliers or announce yourselves on the Internet and let them know you're available to play whenever or wherever.

My True Home

I ARRIVED AT THE AIRPORT with the most excited feeling, walking around looking for the gate so I could board the plane. I felt very enthusiastic about my trip to New York, where in fact I used to live for a short period of my life. I walked through the airport passing by fast food places. I hadn't eaten since I was at home, but not wanting to show up late to the gate and thinking of all the fun I was going to have, I completely forgot I was even hungry. As I sat on my seat on the plane, I decided to sleep. It felt more like I slept for five minutes, while out of the blue the plane arrived in New York. I got out of the plane and walked out of the airport and finally saw my uncle. When he saw me, he greeted me with a huge "Yo!" followed by a hug.

The next few days I spent with my family, going from house to house. In one day I probably went to four houses, since I have family all over New York, mostly Long Island. As I visited most of them, the smiles of their faces filled me with joy. Most of them I haven't seen in years. I enjoyed seeing each and every one of them. I was especially excited to see my dad's side of the family.

As the week was ending, I felt bored, but not from being in New York. It was the feeling of knowing that I had to leave soon, which is disappointing. I enjoyed my trip and was already thinking of my next trip back as soon as possible.

On my last day, as I walked into the deli, I heard all my people speaking the same slang as me. I realized I was home here. Then I turned around and noticed that the slang they used is Salvadorian street talk, like the way gangs talk, but it's just the vocabulary. I smelled the good food: chicken covered in red sauce with different types of rice, also the tortillas freshly made; it was that warm aroma that caught my nose's attention. Afterward my stomach started rumbling; I got really hungry. As I was in town, I realized that I did not want to go back home. Home is where the heart is at, and my heart is in New York.

Open Letter

To our society,

Nobody is born racist. In this world, most emotional things are influenced by hatred or love. We learn these things from close friends and people around us—you have to be careful, because it can be your own family. You have to be prepared to stand out from the bad crowd when you know what is right.

For example, somebody in your family could have a deep hate for someone from another country and/or of another color, and it could influence their younger family members who are learning about the world and curious about how things work. To them, the adults know what is right from wrong.

In my life, I've experienced certain people's ignorance toward my people, and it influenced me in a bad way. But it is a waste of time; hatred toward another people is a waste of energy. I have witnessed racism toward people from my country at a party. A group of guys were talking trash. I got mad and reacted in contempt. I'm not gaining anything out of despising back—it is just a cycle of hate. Hatred can be found anywhere; I've experienced it at work and school.

To find the good in other people, participate in activities you have common interests in. Get to know the person, how they've grown up, and what they've experienced. Respect is the key to better friendships. You earn respect through hard work, caring for other people, friendliness, and being there for those who are worth it. Communication is the most important thing in friendships. It helps you understand where people come from, what they've experienced. It could be possible that all the hatred you have will just die out if you build a friendship with someone from a different society.

I hope people can view these instances as ways to influence new and creative things in the world.

All the best,

Bryan

Nicole Asencio

 Nicole Asencio was born in Ypsilanti, Michigan. She speaks English and Spanish. Her favorite food is burgers. Nicole loves to play with her little sister Joselyn. When she grows up she wants to be an artist.

AGE 9

Recipe for Spaghetti

INGREDIENTS

- Large bowl
- Hot water
- Noodles

DIRECTIONS

1. First, you get a large bowl.
2. Next, you put in hot water.
3. Then, you put in the noodles.
4. After that, you wait for the water to boil.
5. After that, you put in the sauce and ingredients.
6. Last, you put it on the plate and then eat it.

Pen-pal Letters

Dear pen-pal,

My name is Nicole. I am nine years old. My languages are English and Spanish. I have a pet dog at home that is half Chihuahua and half weiner dog. I live in a brick house. My school name is Adams STEM Academy. My favorite teacher is Ms. Chenier. My favorite colors are pink, aqua green, and purple. I have my parents, two twins, big sister, little sister, my baby brother, and me. My birthday is May 29. What's your name? Who's your favorite teacher? Are you a boy or a girl? Is there a lot of work in high school? Do you have friends? What grade are you in? What do you want to be when you grow up?

Sincerely,

Nicole

Dear Nicole,

My name is Bryan. I am seventeen years old and, just like you, my languages are English and Spanish. I have a Chihuahua. She is fluffy but with a pitbull attitude. My birthday is in May, too. Mine is May 8. I have two favorite teachers, Ms. Manier, my chemistry teacher, and Ms. Sirman, my English teacher. In high school, yes, sometimes there is a lot of work, but it is not hard. I'm in the University Small Learning Community, and we get less homework than the STEM students here, but I rarely ever get homework, almost never, since I finish it in class. Yeah, I have a lot of friends in school and out of school, some of them are like brothers to me. My favorite color is red. I love music and can't be without it. I am Salvadorean. Where are your parents from? I am in the eleventh grade. When I grow up, I am going to be working on cars, like fixing them when they are crashed or something. What is your favorite movie? Do you like sports? What do you like to do? What do you want to be when you grow up?

Sincerely,

Bryan

....

Dear Bryan,

I am nine years old. I like your handwriting. It is so neat. My mom is from Honduras. My dad is from Guatemala. My favorite movie is *Underdog*. Yes, I do like sports. Mine is soccer. I like to paint. I want to be an artist when I grow up. What is your favorite sport? What kind of music do you like? Where are your parents from? My favorite tradition is Christmas because I love presents. I love "What Does the Fox Say?" What is your favorite music?

Sincerely,

Nicole

Dear Nicole,

My favorite sport is also soccer, even though I don't like to play it, just to watch it professionally. My favorite team is Barcelona. Real Madrid is trash to me. My favorite music is reggaeton and *bachata*. My parents are from El Salvador. I don't really have traditions. I just celebrate whatever holiday is around. What do you like to do on the weekends? What do you do after school?

Sincerely,

Bryan

....

Dear Bryan,

What I love to do on weekends is go to the mall so I can play on the bounce houses there. After school, we do engineering club on Wednesdays. What do you do on weekends? Do you do anything after school? I love to cook with my family. My mom and dad are the only ones who I cook with. I love to cook food with them. I love to eat with my family, too. I love the snow. Do you love snow?

Sincerely,

Nicole

Dear Nicole,

I hate snow just because I drive to school, and it makes driving really difficult. On the weekends I work, so that means I don't spend much time at home. What else do you do on the weekends? I would cook, but I'm too lazy to cook so I just go out to eat. What do you like to cook? What's your favorite food?

Sincerely,

Bryan

....

Dear Bryan,

That is true about the snow; that always happens when my dad tries to park his car at our house. Also on the weekends I spend time playing with my big sister, Tany, and my little sister, Joselyn. I don't know how to cook, but my mom is teaching me, and the only thing I know how to do is make smoothies. The ingredients in the smoothie are ice cubes, milk, and whatever kinds of fruits. I wish I could cook some burgers right now. My favorite food is burgers. How is your school like a family? My school is like a family because we are nice to each other and we do projects together. We also have great teachers. And we work together to do math. How do you make your school like a family? At Adams, we make our school like a family by respecting each other.

Sincerely,

Nicole

Dear Nicole,

That's nice that you spend time with your sisters, a bond with siblings is very important. I love smoothies. I make them anytime I want, but making them is just the fun part. The school here isn't really like a family; everyone here is on their own—people concentrate on their grades. Yeah, there are a lot of groups of friends, but once they step out of the building they forget about each other; that's how high school is. How's the food at your school? How long is it? How many friends do you have?

Sincerely,

Bryan

....

Dear Bryan,

The food at my school is great, and sometimes they make food that doesn't taste good. I don't know how long because I don't know time. I have a lot of friends. On Tuesdays I do gymnastics. Do you have any specials that are your favorite? What's your favorite dessert?

Sincerely,

Nicole

ALI RAMLAWI

PRESENTS

JERUSALEM GARDEN LENTIL SOUP

Ali Ramlawi is the owner of Jerusalem Garden, a family-owned restaurant serving high-quality Mediterranean food to a loyal Ann Arbor fanbase for more than twenty-five years. Ali took over the full-time management of his family's small Middle Eastern restaurant and helped it grow into the culinary institution it is now known as locally. His family recipes attract thousands of dedicated diners to his restaurant each week, and, as a result, Ali has earned the loving nickname "Falafel King of Ann Arbor."

Jerusalem Garden's lentil soup, which is easy to make and extremely nutritious, is the ultimate comfort food. The ease of storing leftovers and reheating later makes it even better.

Prep time: Forty-five minutes

Serves five to eight

INGREDIENTS

- 2 cups whole red lentils
- 2 teaspoons kosher salt
- 1 teaspoons turmeric
- ½ teaspoon ground cumin
- 1 lemon sliced into eight wedges

DIRECTIONS

1. Wash lentils in lukewarm water three to four times, then drain all water.

2. Combine lentils, salt, turmeric, and cumin into a 4-quart pot.

3. Add 6 cups of cold water and place on a high heat source for fifteen to twenty minutes, stirring occasionally.

4. When lentils begin to break down and turn yellow, lower the heat source to medium-low for fifteen to twenty minutes, stirring often.

5. When lentils have completely broken down, leave soup on a simmer for an additional ten minutes.

6. Serve with a slice of lemon.

Badiarra Maguiraga

Badiarra Maguiraga is fourteen years old. He's from Mali. He was born in New York in 1999, and he grew up in Mali-Bamako, in West Africa. After thirteen years, he came back to the United States to study at Ypsilanti Community High School. He used to like soccer, but now he likes basketball because it's fun and there is no tackling. Badiarra's dream is to be an engineer and to work at NASA controlling space ships.

AGE 14

How to Make Eggs

I love cooking eggs for breakfast, and I love a good recipe for that. The eggs are from my grandpa's chickens. We also took tomatoes and onions from my grandpa's garden,

INGREDIENTS

- 3 eggs
- Oil

- Sliced onion
- 1 tomato in slices

- Pinch of salt
- The essential utensil is the pan

DIRECTIONS

First of all, you have to put oil in the pan; wait five or six seconds with the stove on to make the oil hot. And then you crack three eggs into the pan. Also, cut the tomatoes and the onions in slices. After five seconds, put these in the pan and wait one minute until it is ready. Take off the eggs from the pan, put on the plate, and take some bread and eat it.

My Accident

LAST YEAR, WHEN I WAS IN MALI, I was walking back to class after gym with my friend. A gray car suddenly appeared behind us and hit my friend and me. People took us to the hospital. When I woke up, the first thing I tried to do was stand up, but my mom pushed me back down. I asked her what happened. She said, "Nothing."

Then I said, "If there is nothing, let me stand up."

She said, "No."

I said, "Okay, I'm going to stand up." That's when she told me I had broken both of my legs and my left arm.

The whole place smelled like medicine, and that's how I knew I wasn't in my room. I realized I was in the hospital. When I couldn't stand up, I became angry and cried. After I woke up, they brought me on the plane to the United States because the doctors of the United States are better than African doctors. One year later, I am no longer injured. And now I can't wait to get strong and play basketball again.

Open Letter

Dear YCHS teachers,

To build a stronger community at YCHS, I have some ideas. I think we need more cooperation between teachers and students. We need clear consequences in the classroom, and more teachers so there can be fewer students in class, and we also need more classroom participation. I'm giving you this advice because I'm one of your students, and because I have been here for three semesters. After the first semester, nothing has changed so you all have to talk to the principal for that. I think these are some things you can do better:

· Encourage more participation in classroom

· Teachers talk too fast; please slow down

· Give less homework

· Try to be clear when you are talking

You're good at controlling the class. You are encouraging students to work. Your homework is easy to understand. I think if you follow my advice, there will be more cooperation in class.

Sincerely,

Badiarra Maguiraga

Losany Doumbouya

 Losany was born in Ypsilanti. He has lived there his whole life. His favorite food is fried chicken. His favorite game to play at free time is basketball. He likes to watch basketball and football. He speaks Mandingo and English. His parents are from West Africa. He wants to be a basketball player when he grows up.

AGE 10

Recipe for Fried Chicken

INGREDIENTS

- Chicken
- Flour
- Oil

- Bowl
- Plates
- Pan

- Hot sauce

DIRECTIONS

1. First, you get the chicken out of the refrigerator.
2. You put the flour on the chicken to make it crispy.
3. You let the oil boil.
4. Then, you drop the chicken in the pan, one by one.
5. Then, you wait.
6. Then, you get a bowl and put the chicken in it.
7. Turn the stove off.
8. Eat it with hot sauce.

Pen-pal Letters

Dear Losany,

My name is Badiarra. I am fourteen years old. My favorite color is yellow. I don't have a pet. I'm a tenth grader. My favorite subject is science. I'm a boy. I like books. My favorite book is *Always Running*. I speak Mandingo. I have two sisters. How old are you? What grade are you in? I am from Mali.

Sincerely,

Badiarra

Dear Badiarra,

I am ten years old. I am in the fifth grade. My cousin is from Mali. I have a pet cat. What is your favorite movie or show? Were you born in Michigan? I think your last name is hard to say? I was born in Michigan. My favorite books are SpongeBob books. I celebrate Eid. That's when all Muslims come to one place and they give kids money. And it's all around the world. I made a lot of money. My mom gave me three or four dollars. What did you do for Thanksgiving? I ate turkey and mashed potatoes. I am really good at math.

Sincerely,

Losany

....

Dear Losany,

My favorite show is *Family Guy*. I was born in New York. I celebrate Eid, too.

Sincerely,

Badiarra

....

Dear Badiarra,

What is your favorite food? Do you like SpongeBob? The food I really like is fried chicken. My mom makes it a lot. I like to put hot sauce on it. Do you eat rice? Because I do sometimes. I like my chicken crispy and crunchy. I watch *SpongeBob SquarePants* a lot. It's cool and funny. Bye!

Sincerely,

Losany

Dear Losany,

My favorite food is Chinese food. :) I used to like *SpongeBob SquarePants*. And yes, I do like rice :) but with shrimp. I play soccer. What sport do you like or play?

Sincerely,

Badiarra

....

Dear Badiarra,

My favorite sport I like to play is basketball. We can improve our school by getting to know each other better. And I wish we didn't have uniforms because I don't really like it. I think if we go to each other's classes, we can know each other better. What can you improve about your school? How is your school like a family?

Sincerely,

Losany

Dear Losany,

My school is not like a family. It's like a friend and a friend talking to each other. And it's boring. The only thing that is good is ELL. What is your favorite place in all the world? Mine is Dubai. Who's your favorite teacher? Mine's Ms. Sirman. Is your school fun? If it is, how? My school is not fun because we don't even watch movies. Do you have a bedtime? We don't.

Sincerely,

Badiarra

....

Dear Badiarra,

Why is your school boring? My favorite teacher is Ms. Fitzgerald; she's nice. I think you should go to a better school. And what is Dubai? A city, state, or country? My class had a play about a bus boycott. Do you know Miguel? He's my friend's pen-pal. And do you know Kaleb? His nickname is Joseph.

Losany

BEE ROLL

PRESENTS

SPICY POTATO PARMESAN SOUP

Bee Roll is the owner of beezy's cafe in Ypsilanti, a restaurant celebrating simple, fresh, locally-sourced food. Having lived all over the United States, Bee brings her traveling experience to bear on the menu at beezy's, all with the goal of serving good food to a community she now calls home.

This is the first soup I ever created in the spring of 1999, pregnant with my eldest daughter. I'd just discovered Sriracha. I love making soup because it's easy to experiment with flavors that might not ordinarily go together. For example, Sriracha, while now ubiquitous in restaurants, was once just used in Vietnamese cooking, and parmesan is usually associated with Italian cooking. There's not a lot of Italian-Vietnamese fusion cooking, but the creaminess of cheese and the heat of chili garlic sauce accented by sweet carrots, tangy sour cream, and hefty butter satisfy the belly in ways no other soup I make can. Or, I'm just really attached to this recipe since it was my first creation.

Serves about ten (1 gallon)

INGREDIENTS

- 8 small red potatoes, scrubbed and diced, leave peels on—set aside covered in cool water
- 3-4 medium carrots, peeled and chopped
- 1 small onion, diced
- 2 stalks celery
- 1 stick butter

- 2 cloves minced garlic
- 1 cup flour
- 2 cups cold water
- A good whisk and five minutes of absolute concentration
- 2-4 tablespoons soup base (paste or bouillon)
- 4 more cups cold water

- 2 teaspoons each of oregano and basil
- 1 cup shredded or grated parmesan
- 2 tablespoons Sriracha sauce
- 1 cup sour cream
- 4 cups milk
- Black pepper

DIRECTIONS

1. In a saucepan, cook celery, carrots, and onion in butter until vegetables are soft, then add garlic and cook another minute or two.

2. Add flour and cook five minutes over low heat. Do not brown and work to make sure the flour is cooking evenly; you want to just cook the flour enough to take on a slightly nutty flavor but not get too deep. Whisk in two cups cold water, pouring water with one hand while the other is whisking, incorporating all the flour. Your vegetables will break up a bit too! Pay attention to the bottom and sides of pot to get all the flour magic in there. Keep heat at medium low and, within a few minutes, the mixture will thicken enough to coat the back of a spoon. As it starts to thicken, add the additional four cups water in intervals to maintain a thickish consistency. Add the base, herbs, and parmesan cheese. Keep cooking on low heat until cheese is incorporated. (This will now be referred to as "the roux.")

3. In another pot, cook the potatoes until fork-tender. Drain, but keep some of that potato water if you want (no more than a cup). Depending on which pot you like better or which has more room, add your potatoes to the roux or the roux over the potatoes. Stir to combine. (By now you've let go of your whisk and are using a wooden spoon or similar instrument.)

4. Add the Sriracha sauce and sour cream and incorporate, then add milk to desired consistency; heat through and add a pinch of black pepper. Serve in ten-ounce bowls with some crusty bread and a salad, and live the good life.

Ghinwa Mikdashi

 Ghinwa Mikdashi was born on July 22, 1997, in Beirut, Lebanon. She's of medium height and is a sixteen-year-old girl who spends her time singing, babysitting, laughing, and listening to music. But that's not what her goal in life is: Ghinwa's goal is to graduate from high school and go to college. Her dream is to be a pediatrician because she really loves kids and cares about them, and likes to play with them.

AGE 16

Recipe for *Moghrabieh*

My favorite dish is *moghrabieh*, a Lebanese food. It reminds me of home. My mom cooks it on special occasions like Eid, a holiday that's all about sharing. It's so good that you will never want to stop eating it. It contains the taste of cinnamon. To make it special, I add cumin to the chicken. After you cook the chicken, you cut it into pieces and put them on the *moghrabieh*.

Estimated time: One hour

MATERIALS

- 1 tablespoon sugar
- 1 pound dry *moghrabieh*
- 1 can cooked chickpeas
- 1½ tablespoons ground caraway

- 1 tablespoon ground cinnamon
- Salt and pepper to taste
- 1 cinnamon stick
- 1 bay leaf
- 1 carrot

- Olive oil or clarified butter
- 1 whole chicken, weighing three pounds
- ¼ cup cumin for flavoring the chicken

ROAST CHICKEN DIRECTIONS

1. Wash and dry the chicken.
2. Place a cinnamon stick, bay leaf, and a chopped carrot inside the chicken.
3. Sprinkle cumin on the outside of the chicken.
4. Roast the chicken at 325°F for one hour.

MOGHRABIEH DIRECTIONS

1. The first step is to heat 8 cups of water with 1 tablespoon of sugar.
2. Wait for the water to boil, and then add the bag of *moghrabieh* to the pot.
3. Bring to second boil, wait until *moghrabieh* gets soft and puffed up. Drain the extra water.
4. Mix together the caraway, cinnamon, salt, and pepper in a small bowl.
5. Mix the *moghrabieh* with the mixed spices.
6. Add the chickpeas.
7. Cut pieces of chicken and put them on top of the *moghrabieh*.

Story of my Life

I WAS BORN IN LEBANON ON JULY 22, 1997. My sister was born ahead of me by five minutes. My brother came a year before both of us. We grew up with one another and with our cousins.

We all went to Bach School together. My sister and I went in third grade. My brother and cousins went in the fifth grade together. It was a good experience going there. We all had fun and learned a lot.

I spent my childhood in Ann Arbor. I played with my cousins, brother, and sister. We used to buy fireworks and play with the sprinkler in the front yard. It's a house that I'll always remember.

We traveled back to Lebanon on July 22. A couple nights passed, and we started to hear planes and gunshots. We turned on the TV and heard that a ship was coming to take all Americans back to the US. We packed our stuff and headed to the dock.

In the summer of 2013, my brother, sister, and I decided to go to the US for school and to see our family. So we told our parents, then they got the tickets. Our plane left on July 1. I was so hyped and excited to travel, but the thing that disappointed me was leaving my parents and friends. All our friends came on the day that we were going to travel. So we talked and laughed for hours. My brother and his friends were in one group, and my sister and I were in another.

It was time to go; saying goodbye was the hardest thing ever. At the airport, I started to cry a lot. When we got in the secure area, I started crying more because I saw my mom and dad go farther and farther away. It was the saddest moment ever.

I hope in the future to graduate from high school and be a pediatrician. I love kids, especially my baby cousin, Malik. He's the cutest baby cousin ever, and his sister Amira is very adorable, too.

Starbucks Paradise

F OR A VACATION, MY FAMILY AND I planned to go to the Motor City Hotel. As a first step, I prepared all the clothes and folded them together and packed them with my eye make-up. I felt so excited and hyped for spending the night there because of the comfy beds, the Starbucks store downstairs, and the computer labs. Yasmin, my helpful cousin, started washing the dishes, and Farah, the quiet one, cleaned the house because we wanted the house clean and neat before leaving it. My tall brother Hasan took out the garbage and vacuumed the floor. My aunt Esmat started preparing the bags with me. When I finished everything, I helped my grandma to get dressed.

When I first arrived at the Motor City Hotel, I was so thrilled and amazed by the big building and the parking lot full of cars. When we got in, our family checked into our rooms and got dressed up for the buffet. The most exciting moment that happened was when all five of us went down to the cafe and bought Starbucks. It was exciting because when we ran down the hallway; we felt like we were children running down to the playground.

When we got home, I felt exhausted. But if they told me to pack my stuff again, I would run and be the first one in the car, although I was so tired. Going to the Motor City Hotel is a wonderful memory and a day to remember!

Open Letter

Dear Ypsilanti Community School leaders,

In order to make our school a greater community, I have some ideas to improve it.

First, our lunchroom is too crowded and busy. It's full and it looks like a zoo. There are too many fights and too much cussing in the hallways; we sometimes don't feel friendly and safe. There should be more respect between students and teachers, because the students don't have the right to talk to the teachers that way.

I'm qualified to be someone who's giving advice to the school because I'm a member of this community and it's important for my education. My experience of coming from another country to the US has taught me to learn and fit in. It taught me how to make friends and be friendly. My ELL class is very friendly and funny. I like it because we're all close to one another, and we are a family.

One of the things YCHS does well is the bus system. Each bus has its number on it, and the students who ride it know their number. I also like that there are no uniforms because each person has the freedom to chose what they wear. Finally, some of the teachers let us use our phones while doing our work, during the free time, and in the hallways. I think letting us have our freedom is a good thing.

The school should work on hiring more security guards because the hallways are always crowded. The students who are not willing to study and learn should be expelled. More lunchrooms should be added because the lines are so long and people aren't able to get their lunch. I hope our school leaders will make decisions for more freedom and safety and fewer fights.

Sincerely,

Ghinwa

Danat Tadese

 Danat Tadese was born in Ypsilanti, Michigan. She speaks African and English. Her favorite food is Ethiopian food. Danat plays with her big sister. When Danat grows up she wants to be a doctor.

AGE 9

Pen-pal Letters

Dear pen-pal,

My name is Danat. I am nine years old. My favorite subject is math. My favorite colors are purple, blue, and pink, and my teacher's name is Ms. Chenier. My language is African and my favorite movies are *Shake it Up* and *Jessie*. My school is Adams. My favorite pets are cats and dogs. My favorite book is *Sassy: The Birthday Storm*, and my favorite sport is gymnastics. And I have one brother. What grade are you in? What's your name? What is your favorite teacher? What is your favorite movie? Where are you from? What are you going to be when you grow up?

Sincerely,

Danat

Dear Danat,

My name is Ghinwa, and I'm from Lebanon. I'm sixteen years old and I'm in the tenth grade. I have a brother and a sister. My sister and I are fraternal twins. I'm older than her by five minutes. My brother is older than us; he's seventeen, so he's a senior. It's his last year in high school. My teacher's name is Ms. Sirman. She teaches me English. My favorite teacher is my ROTC teacher. ROTC stands for Reserve Officer Training Corps, so we learn how to march, to salute, we do physical training, and we have our own uniforms. My ROTC teacher's name is Sergeant John Guyer, but we call him "Sarge." I like him because he's funny and stands up for himself. My favorite movies are *Shutter Island*, *The Great Gatsby*, *The Notebook*, and many more. My favorite colors are blue and purple. When I grow up I want to be a pediatrician. It's a doctor for children. I look forward to writing back and forth with you.

Ghinwa

....

Dear Ghinwa,

Thank you for your letter, Ghinwa. I really enjoyed your letter. Do you have a favorite pet? My favorite pets are dogs and cats. I am so excited for Christmas. Every year my family and I go to Virginia to celebrate Christmas. What do you do for the holiday? I am really looking forward to talking with you.

From,

Danat

Dear Danat,

You are more than welcome, and I enjoyed your letter as well. My favorite pet is a dog, and I am very excited for Christmas, too. In Lebanon we don't celebrate it, we just do a family dinner and that's it. But here in America, we do, but this year we won't because my aunt and brother traveled to Lebanon because an emergency happened at home. So it's just me, my sister, my two cousins, and my grandma living in the house. When they come back, we will celebrate and make a family dinner. But we will just put the decorations and the tree together. What do you want for Christmas? And what country in Africa are you from? I'm looking forward to your response.

From,

Ghinwa

....

Dear Ghinwa,

My family is from Ethiopia, and what I want for Christmas is a dog and a cat because they're fun to play with. For Christmas, my family and I are going to Virginia, and all my family is going to eat dinner together and we're going to eat Ethiopian food, and it is very spicy to eat. And my mom is going to make the food. What do you do special?

Sincerely,

Danat

Dear Danat,

I spent my Christmas at my older cousin's house. I slept there and we stayed up until two o'clock in the morning. When we woke up we opened our presents, and I got two new cases for my phone—a blue one and a pink one. Then we ate breakfast: hash browns, bacon, and eggs. My favorite foods are Chinese food and tuna salad.

<3, Ghinwa

....

Dear Ghinwa,

I think you had fun at your cousin's house! On the weekend, my friends and I are going to Chuck E. Cheese's because it is my little sister's birthday, and she is turning three years old, and my friends and I are going to the movie theater and I do not know what movie we're going to watch. Do you like going to the movies? Did you see some movies before? What kind of movies did you see? I like going to the movie theater with my friends because we can see the same movie and we can talk about the movie after the movie ends and have a sleepover.

Sincerely,

Danat

ARI WEINZWEIG

PRESENTS

PIMENTO CHEESE

Ari Weinzweig is a founding partner
and co-owner of Zingerman's Community
of Businesses and author of six books,
including *Zingerman's Guide to Better Bacon* and
Zingerman's Guide to Good Leading Part 2,
A Lapsed Anarchist's Approach to Being a Better
Leader. In 2006, Ari was recognized as one
of the "Who's Who of Food & Beverage in
America" by the James Beard Foundation,
an organization dedicated to celebrating
American culinary tradition.

While everyone in the South knows this stuff at a level of intimacy my family would have reserved for chopped liver, it's still relatively unheard of up here in the North.

Small slices of toast, spread with pimento cheese, and topped with a bit of crisp bacon, if you like, and a leaf or two of celery, make a superb appetizer. Pimento cheese sandwiches with bacon and tomato are terrific, too. I like them grilled, but they're actually very good toasted, as well.

We make a pimento cheese macaroni and cheese at the Roadhouse that's at its best topped with chopped bits of crisp bacon. This is also outstanding on a burger—not really melted, just softened up a bit from the heat of the meat. If that's where you're headed, I'd go for a couple of slices of Arkansas-peppered bacon, along with a little bit of chopped celery leaf to lighten the whole thing up just a touch.

INGREDIENTS

- ½ pound sharp cheddar, coarsely grated (We use the two-year-old raw milk cheddar from Grafton Village.)
- 1 cup mayonnaise (I prefer Hellmann's up here; out west, the same mayo is sold under the brand name Best Foods.)
- ¼ cup diced roasted red peppers
- ¾ teaspoon olive oil
- ¼ teaspoon freshly ground Tellicherry black pepper
- Scant ¼ teaspoon cayenne pepper, or to taste
- Pinch coarse sea salt

DIRECTIONS

1. Fold all the ingredients together in a mixing bowl.
2. Mix well.
3. Eat.
4. Repeat as regularly as you like.

It's addictive: as more than one person around here has said more than once, "It's kind of good on pretty much everything, isn't it?"

Serves . . . well, it's kind of hard to say. A real addict could probably consume this entire recipe in a single sitting. Being more conservative, let's say it's enough to serve eight as an appetizer. You'll probably have to test it on your family and friends to see how much they can eat!

Excerpted from *Zingerman's Guide to Better Bacon*

Nadine Mikdashi

 Nadine Mikdashi is from Lebanon. She is sixteen years old. She was born on July 22, 1997. She used to live with her parents, but now she lives in the USA with her aunt and cousins. Her mom, Abir, is here for one month. Nadine's nickname is Dino. Her favorite color is pink, and she wants to work in a bank. She loves to shop, dance, swim, and sing. She has a sister, her fraternal twin, Ghinwa, who's older by five minutes. She has an older brother named Hasan who's seventeen years old. She is a sophomore at Ypsilanti Community High School.

AGE 16

How to Babysit my Cousins

Babysitting is fun, but it's exhausting if you are babysitting more than one kid. Here are some good tips for babysitting. My sister babysits my cousins. She stays with them the whole time. I watch them play, my sister feeds them, and every time their parents come home, they cry because they don't want to leave. So they usually stay for one night. Here is what I learned from my sister babysitting my cousins.

Estimated time: One to two hours

MATERIALS

- Baby powder
- Food: bananas, oranges, cheese, bagels, cereals, Oreos, yogurt (*laban*), rice, pancakes, waffles, eggs, fries, ice cream, candy, pop, milk, peaches, apples, chicken, toast, cream cheese, grapes
- Clothes: jacket, hat, pants, shoes (Nike), underwear, pajamas, blankets
- Toys: balls, swing, slides, Playstation, phones
- Bathtub
- Diapers
- Lotion
- Medicine
- Stories
- Books (princess books)

DIRECTIONS

1. First, you help them out by playing outside with the swings and slides by pushing them. If they're hurt, you're responsible.

2. Sit them at the table. Feed them a bowl of yogurt, rice, oranges, and a glass of milk because they like them and because they're healthy foods.

3. Undress them and put them in a bathtub to take a bath. When they are done, gently put some lotion on their bodies because it smells good and because it's clean.

4. Put their clothes on (pants, underwear, t-shirt, sleeves, jacket).

5. Read them a bedtime story (princess story) to make them fall asleep.

6. Take them to bed by lifting them up gently.

How to Make Grape Leaves

On the weekend, my family makes a big dinner full of Lebanese food like tabouli, falafel, chicken, hummus, rice, shawarma, and grape leaves. We sit together and enjoy our meal. We talk about if there is a problem in the house, we joke and laugh, and we talk about food. My aunt cooks all the Lebanese food, and I help her. This makes me miss my mom because she cooks in Lebanon, and, every time we come home from school, I smell the food.

Estimated time: About an hour

INGREDIENTS

- 1 cup olive oil
- 2 lemons
- 3 cups water
- 2 teaspoons salt
- 2 cups rice
- 5 mint leaves
- 1 cup ground meat
- 2 small onions
- 1 teaspoon pepper

DIRECTIONS

1. Cook the ground meat and onions on the stove with oil.

2. Mix the rice, ground meat, pepper, salt, and onions together.

3. Fold the grape leaves with the ingredients.

4. Dip them in olive oil for a good taste.

5. Put them in the pot full of boiling water in order to cook them for thirty minutes.

6. Finally, put the grape leaves on a plate and add lemon and mint as a garnish.

7. Enjoy the recipe and sit with your family.

Me, Myself, and I

MY NAME IS NADINE MIKDASHI. I am sixteen years old. I was born on July 22, 1997. I live with my cousins, parents, brother, and grandmother. My old school was Khaled Binalwalid Ihoroj. In 2006, there was a war in Lebanon, so my family and I traveled to the United States by ship. The airport was closed, and we spent two or three days to get here. The first stop was from Lebanon to Ethiopia and then Ethiopia to the United States. On the second day, it was my sister Ghinwa's and my birthday. The army men lifted us into the air and everyone sang "Happy Birthday." On the ship, I saw white jellyfish. I smelled the salty sea. The birds sounded like they were singing a song.

We lived in Ann Arbor on Dexter Road. It was a great place. It was peaceful and quiet. We played with the neighbors and watched a lot of movies back then. We still do. That house was bigger. I loved it more than the new one on Dupont.

We have a lot of memories there. When it snowed for the first time, I was shocked, and we played in it and threw snowballs. The snow was as white as an old man's beard.

My cousins and I were registered at Bach Elementary. I really loved my friends. I was with them in class in third grade. They were cool and fun to hang out with. I remember a few of them, but not a lot, and I really miss them. When we went back to Lebanon, they wrote a big card for me saying that they were going to miss me and to have a safe flight. I never saw that card, but my cousin told me about it.

We went back to Lebanon because my parents had work there and the war had ended. We went back to our country and stayed there for three years.

Now I am in the United States again, and my parents are still in Lebanon because of work. We're here because of school. I really like it here, but I miss my parents and my friends. Our school is called Ypsilanti Community High School. The reason that it's called "community" is because Willow Run joined our school. The school is awesome. We get to wear anything we want, including nail polish. And there's a prom, a homecoming dance, a winter ball, and a military ball. Those are what I'm most excited about. In contrast, the schools in Lebanon were more strict. We wore uniforms, weren't allowed to wear colored clothes, and there was no fighting.

In four months, I'm going back to Lebanon. I am thrilled about going to Lebanon because I want to see my parents and friends.

Looking back into my memories of my childhood, I think my life has been exciting and interesting. I hope in the future there are more memorable experiences to enjoy.

A Cold Night

I WAS EXCITED FOR THIS HALLOWEEN because I was going to get free candy from our neighbors. I was ready to go out, so I got dressed like Gretchen, a girl from Switzerland. Yasmine, Imad, Hasan, Christina, Rami, Ghinwa, Amira, Victoria, and I went trick-or-treating around the neighborhood to get some candy in the cold weather. It was dark and rainy. All of us were freezing. My cousins and I walked a lot and got a lot of candy.

At one point, we were walking down the street, and we saw a glowing house. The house was huge and pretty. It had a lot of lights outside and decorations, like ghosts, skeletons, and pumpkins. I didn't think that it was going to be different, but this one was very different from the other houses around it. To ring the doorbell, the old man told us that we had to press the top of the pumpkins' heads in order to open the door. When we went to the front porch, the old couple told us to scream and say trick or treat. That made me happy. We said trick or treat really loudly. I got one Snickers bar and it was the regular size, not the small size. My favorite type of candy is Jolly Ranchers—the blue ones. We got a lot of Jolly Ranchers while trick-or-treating.

After that, all of us were tired and cold because it was raining. My clothes, jacket, hair, and shoes got wet. I really liked the decorations. They were nice and a little bit scary. The neighborhood was full of lights. On our way back home, each one of us opened our bags, and we saw a lot of candy and chocolate. We ate some of it; it tasted delicious, and we saved the rest for later. I wish I could repeat that day but without the rain because it was freezing.

Imad, Yasmine, Hasan, Ghinwa, Rami, Christina, Amira, Victoria, and I enjoyed eating the candy and all of us relaxed after trick-or-treating. We were all exhausted, but it was a fun night. The candy was delicious, but the most important thing was that I felt connected with my cousins and I had a lot of fun. What's really special is that they were with me when I was young. I grew up with my cousins. We were far away from each other, and that's why this was such a special moment.

Open Letter

Dear Ypsilanti Community High School,

I have some advice for how to make this school community stronger. I've noticed some problems in this school: fights, smoking, skipping classes, arguing with teachers, and misbehaving in class. These things are becoming a habit to the students. I want that to stop.

I'm giving the advice because I'm new to this school, and I would like to improve some things in it by helping others get to class on time and do well with grades. I want the school to have more parties, decrease the number of students in lunch, let us listen to music, and for the students who misbehave to stay after school for extra work.

What I like about this school is that they have security guards, because if there's a fight, they will stop it. That's a good thing. What's also better about this school is meeting new friends and wearing colorful clothes because in Lebanon, we wear uniforms. The dances—for instance, Homecoming, Winter Ball, and Prom—are cool because we wear dresses and make-up and get to look more unique.

I hope the school will add some new things and new rules which the students will like and enjoy more.

Sincerely,

Nadine

Melissa Vongphachanh

 Melissa was born in Ypsilanti, Michigan. She lives in Ypsilanti. She speaks Laotian and English. Her favorite food is pasta and Asian food. She likes to paint her nails, listen to music, and spend time with family. When she grows up she wants to be a doctor who helps sick children and who helps sick animals. She also likes to play with small dogs. When she grows up she wants to live in New York City.

AGE 12

Recipe for Nachos

INGREDIENTS

- Shredded cheese
- Salsa

- Tortilla chips or Doritos
- Meat (cook it)

- Sour cream
- Pieces of lettuce

DIRECTIONS

1. Put chips on a plate and add the ingredients of your own on top!
2. Yum!

Pen-pal Letters

Dear pen-pal,

I am in sixth grade. I am also a girl. My name is Melissa. What's your name? I speak Laotian. I attend Adams STEM Academy. I am twelve years old. How old are you? My teacher's name is Mr. Moore. What's your teacher's name? My favorite colors are pink and light blue. Can I know your favorite color? My favorite holidays are Christmas and Thanksgiving. What's yours? How many classes do you take? I don't take much because I'm still in elementary school. I live with three brothers and one sister. Who do you live with? This is the second time I've had a pen-pal. It's very exciting to get one. My favorite pet is a dog. Do you have a favorite pet? When I grow up I want to be a person who helps sick children. I almost forgot to ask you, what languages do you speak?

Sincerely,

Melissa

Dear Melissa,

I am a girl too! My name is Nadine. I speak English and Arabic. I am sixteen years old and I'm in tenth grade. My teacher's name is Ms. Sirman. My favorite colors are pink and aqua blue. I really like your name and your handwriting. My favorite holidays are Christmas, Thanksgiving, Easter, and Halloween. I take six classes. I live with my aunt, sister, brother, two cousins, and my grandma. I have a pet (a dog), and his name is Cocoa. When I grow up, I am going to be a dental hygienist or a model. A dental hygienist is a person who cleans other people's teeth. Oh, and I have some questions to ask you. What's your favorite movie? Who is your favorite singer/actress? What's your last name?

Sincerely,

Nadine

....

Dear Nadine,

My favorite singer is Ariana Grande. Also, my favorite actress would probably be Keke Palmer. Who's yours? My favorite movie is *Despicable Me 2*. My favorite real-person movie is *Fast and Furious*. What's yours? *Fast and Furious* is an action movie. My last name is Vongphachanh (vong)(pha)(chanh). I wondered what do you do for family traditions for Christmas? I go to my cousin's house for Christmas and open presents with my family and play with my cousin. I like painting my nails with different colors. What do you like to do? What's your favorite song? My favorite song is "Neon Lights" by Demi Lovato.

Sincerely,

Melissa

Dear Melissa,

My favorite singer is Demi Lovato. My favorite actor is Ashton Kutcher. My favorite people in movies are Ashton Kutcher and Jennifer Lawrence. I live with my cousins, so I celebrate Christmas with them and we open the presents together, but this year I'm not going to celebrate it because my aunt and my brother are outside of the country. I like to stay on my phone and listen to music all the time. I like to paint my nails too! My favorite song is "Calling You" by Outlandish. It's amazing. You should listen to it. Do you have any brothers and sisters? When's your birthday? What do you do on weekends? I love the tree you drew. What's your favorite food? Do you have any pets? What do you want for Christmas? I want make-up.

Sincerely,

Nadine

....

Dear Nadine,

I actually do have brothers and sisters. I have one sister and three brothers. My birthday is on February 4. When's your birthday? On the weekend, I don't really do much. I sometimes go over to my grandma's house and go grocery shopping. What do you do on the weekend? The tree that I drew was not that great to me, but thank you. I like cooking all kinds of food with my mom. Most of all I like cooking spaghetti. Sometimes I go out and eat with my family at the buffet. Where do you go out to eat? What do you like to cook? Yes, I do have a pet. His name is Norbit, and he is a dog. For Christmas I want nail polish and really cute boots. What is your food experience?

Sincerely,

Melissa

Mariana Ovalle

 Mariana Ovalle was born on May 19. She is from Mexico, and now she is a student at Ypsilanti Community High School. She loves to play soccer and enjoy good times with her family. Mariana likes to play video games with her brothers, friends, and boyfriend. She plans to graduate from high school and go to Eastern Michigan University. Her dream is to become a good nurse and help others.

AGE 18

Recipe for Christmas *Ponche*

This delicious Mexican *Ponche* has natural and healthy ingredients. All the people from my little town in Mexico love to make it for the Christmas holidays. It's a traditional food for holidays. It's a good feeling when you drink it. For the people who like wine, you can add it, like my father always does at our holidays in December. So do the rest of my family who love to drink it when we are eating tamales.

Estimated time: Forty-five minutes

MATERIALS:

- 5 guavas
- ½ of a sugar cane
- 5 tamarinds
- 1 liter water
- Sugar (all that you want)
- 2 or 3 apples
- Container
- Spoon
- Stove
- Knife

DIRECTIONS:

1. First, you have to wash and cut the sugar cane into big pieces and the guava and apples into medium slices.

2. Boil water and put a lid on it.

3. When the water is boiling, add the ingredients (sugar, sugar cane, and fruit).

4. Let it boil for half an hour. Enjoy!

An *Agradable* Reunion with My Family

Aᴛᴛᴇʀ ᴀ ʏᴇᴀʀ ᴏꜰ ᴍɪꜱꜱɪɴɢ ᴍʏ ᴛᴡᴏ ꜱɪꜱᴛᴇʀꜱ who had left Mexico to come to the United States, we decided to move to them, and we prepared our trip. I wanted to meet my sisters again, like Romeo and Juliet wanted to be together when their parents separated them.

After our trip from Mexico to the United States of America, we (my mother, my father, my brother Jesús, my brother José, his wife and daughters, and I) started to make tamales for our dinner. My older sister, Alejandra, had a new baby, and I wanted to know him. We prepared everything. We took showers, and we traveled to Ypsilanti, which was thirty minutes away from Wixom, where I was living.

When we stopped in front of my sisters' house, they went out and started kissing and hugging us. We were very happy. Everyone went in the house and we started to tell them about our trip and how it was. My older sister asked me if I was sad about leaving my boyfriend in Mexico, and, actually, I really was. We started to eat the tamales, and my older sister told my mom that she missed her and the way she cooks tamales. My brother turned on a movie from my *quinceañera* so my sisters could watch it because they were not there for my birthday party. We watched the movie and cleaned up. After that, we went to sleep because we were very tired from the trip. I started to think that I have a beautiful family and I don't want to be far away from them because . . . there is no good place if you are not with family.

Open Letter

Dear Ypsilanti Community High School,

I would like to make you aware that we have too many problems with our school. There are people fighting in the hallways, smoking in the bathroom, arguing with teachers in class, skipping classes, using inappropriate language, and we really need to change those things if we want to have a better school for the next generations. We have to do something.

One of my recommendations is to bring more people who can help students during their classes. For example, we have a lot of volunteers in Ms. Sirman's class. If the students in general understand what the teacher talks about, I'm really sure that they will like it, but if they don't, they will start to argue with the teacher, talk with their friends, and use their phones.

We have volunteers from 826michigan who can help us with classwork. That way all the students can have more attention so they can enjoy the classes.

I don't want to make someone feel uncomfortable or upset, but I am a student of this school and I really want to change it. But not in a bad way! I hope we can solve these problems and make it better for our future students, because it will improve our reputation. It would also decrease all the bad things that people know about the school.

Mariana Ovalle

Gisela Romero-Canseco

 Gisela Romero-Canseco was born in Ypsilanti. She speaks Spanish and English. Her favorite food is spaghetti. She wants to be a doctor when she grows up. She likes to read books and color.

AGE 8

Pen-pal Letters

Dear pen-pal,

My name is Gisela. My age is eight. My favorite color is pink. I speak English and Spanish. My favorite subject is math. My teacher is Ms. Simpson. What's your name? How old are you? What is your teacher's name? What's your favorite color? What language do you speak?

Sincerely,

Gisela

Dear Gisela,

I like your name, that's my niece's name. My name is Mariana, I am from Mexico, and I am eighteen years old. My teacher's name is Ms. Sirman. My favorite color is pink, like yours, and I speak Spanish, like you, and my favorite subject is math, too. I work at McDonald's, and I love my job. I'd like to know, where are you from? And how long have you been in the United States of America? What do you like to do after school?

Your friend from high school,

Mariana Ovalle

....

Dear Mariana,

I like your letter. I am from Michigan. I was born in Michigan. After school I like to read books. On Christmas, I get my Christmas tree. What do you do?

From,

Gisela

Dear Gisela,

I love to be with all my family on Christmas because my mother cooks Mexican food and it is delicious, like tamales and other things. Do you like Mexican food? Do you have any brothers or sisters? I have two sisters and three brothers. They all are from Mexico like me, but we all live here in a white house in Ypsilanti, and if you want to come someday, you are welcome to do it. We can play with my little brother and niece. She is eight years old like you, and he is eleven years old. I will like to know more about your family if you want to tell me. :)

Your friend,

Mariana

....

Dear Mariana,

I like Mexican food, too. My sister cooks Mexican food. I have three sisters and three brothers. I live in a white house. My favorite food memory is when my dad buys my birthday cake. Do you have a favorite animal? Do you have a favorite book?

Sincerely,

Gisela

Dear Gisela,

Nice that you like Mexican food, too. My older sister cooks Mexican food deliciously. My favorite animal is a rabbit. I do not like to read too much, but I like the book about Jenni Rivera, a Mexican singer who died a year ago. Do you like to play video games like I do?

Your friend,

Mariana

....

Dear Mariana,

I do not like to play video games. Do you have a pet? My school is like a family because my class knows everyone and we share. How is your school like a family?

From,

Gisela

Dear Gisela,

I do have a pet, but not here. He is in Mexico with my older brother, but we always go to Mexico in December to visit them. My pet's name is Goten. We got the name from *Dragon Ball Z*. All of my brothers and I love *Dragon Ball Z*. I like my school. Almost everyone is nice, but I love my second- and third-hour classes because we all are like a big family; like you guys, we share everything.

Mariana Ovalle

....

Dear Mariana,

What kind of pet do you have? Do you miss him? My birthday is coming up. It is on March 11.

From: Gisela

Sheridan Zaldivar

 Sheridan Zaldivar has been a student at Ypsilanti Community High School for one-and-a-half years. He was born in Mexico in 1997; when he was in childhood he played soccer pick-up games. He has two brothers and three sisters, one beautiful mother, and one father. When he graduates high school, he will work a lot. He wants to work for a landscaping company.

AGE 16

My Best Birthday

HELLO, MY NAME IS SHERIDAN. I will talk about the first day I got on a plane on August 13, 2008, the day of my birthday.

My mom prepared our bags to go to Acapulco for one week, and she ordered a taxi to the airport. My mom is cute. She has black hair, darker than mine, and she understands everything. She gives me too much love; I'm the little one. My mom, my sister Viridiana, and I arrived at the airport and waited for our plane to leave.

After fifteen minutes, we boarded the plane to take off. I felt something I never had felt. It felt like a tickle. When we were in the air, all looked so small, and I felt very happy because it was a new experience. I liked to see the clouds because they looked more real than on the ground. I felt very scared because we descended very quickly, and I felt like the plane was jumping.

When we arrived in Acapulco, it was all very ordered and easy. A taxi took us to go to a fancy, expensive hotel. In the hallways there were aquariums with fish from the ocean. In the hotel I took a shower, and then we went to a restaurant to eat. It looked something like a Red Lobster, but better. I ate a delicious meal of seafood, and after eating we went for a walk to the plaza of Acapulco. Because it was night, there were people dancing and slow beach music with marimbas and torches near the dancers. Then we went back to the hotel and went to sleep.

The next day we went to the beach to swim. We were swimming a long time. The beach was full of *extranjeros* and *vendedores* who were selling coconut juice, homemade bracelets, and fried plantains. There were banana boats floating in the ocean. Then, we went to eat and visit a museum of history and science. I saw dinosaur bones and guns. We spent some time there and then went to dinner at the hotel, and then I took a shower and slept.

The next day, we went to a huge aquarium close to the beach and spent about four hours there. I saw so many fish that I didn't know existed. Some tanks were as big as a room, and some were as small as a microwave. The fish had so many colors, like the rainbow, only stronger. We went for lunch, and we went to spend time downtown for the rest of the day. There was sun all the time. My mom bought a toy for me and my sister. We were very happy. My mom bought a very nice shirt.

My last day of being in Acapulco we went to the beach another time to collect shells. I gathered more than my sister, and my mom swam a little, and then we went to eat and visit at the Port of Acapulco. We went to the downtown; my mom bought me and my sister a bracelet and one shirt. The bracelet had our names written on it, and my mom bought one bracelet. We bought one rose ice cream; it tastes like how it smells. The day was finishing, and we saw the sunset on the beach. The next day, we had to return to Mexico at nine o'clock in the morning. We went to sleep. The next day we went to the airport to return, and I was afraid of the plane.

Everything was wonderful. I loved the holidays with my family. When we got to my home, I went out to play with my friends. They talked of how wonderful my vacation in Acapulco was. My favorite moment was *la puesta de sol, porque fue algo muy bonita, porque nos acostamos a la orilla del mar y vimos completa la puesta del sol*, changing the colors of the enormous, unique sky. *Fue algo muy especial* because my family *estaba junto a mi*.

(My favorite moment was the sunset because it was something very beautiful, because we slept at the edge of the sea, and we saw the entire sunset changing the colors of the enormous, unique sky. It was something very special because my family was close to me.)

Recipe

Isai and Sheridan wrote a recipe together.
You can find it on page 148.

Open Letter

Dear school board,

There are some problems in Ypsilanti Community High School that I would like to discuss and give ideas for improvement. First, lunchtime is a big problem. The lines are too long, and there is not enough time to eat after getting the food. Second, I think detention is a bad idea because I don't learn anything. Finally, there are too many police in the school. I have been in other schools where they don't have security, and it feels more like high school. I think high school is more serious. It is not kindergarten, and having security makes the school have a bad reputation—people think it is a violent school.

To make the school better, we can do some things differently. First, I think the school needs to give more time for lunch because we have too many people in the cafeteria for just thirty minutes. Also, it would be easier to meet other students and to have conversations. Finally, the food should be better, because the food is so greasy. The students will feel better with healthier food and with more time spent together.

In detention, we sit and do nothing for an hour. That time would be better if the students had to do some cleaning or work around the school. Students could help take pride in the school by keeping it clean, picking up garbage outside, or helping plant and take care of flowers.

The security guards don't walk around the school very much, and, when people fight, they are usually in the office, which is not good. So, it might be better if they had a camera system in the office that the security guards can monitor. Then, the high school wouldn't look like a jail, but the security would be able to respond quickly if there were a problem.

Please consider my ideas to make Ypsilanti Community High School a stronger school.

Sincerely,

Sheridan Zaldivar

Katie Joraka

 Katie Joraka was born in Ypsilanti, Michigan. She speaks Thai, English, and Laotian. Her favorite food is Thai. Katie Joraka loves to play with Tay Tay. She wants to be a teacher when she grows up.

AGE 9

Pen-pal Letters

Dear pen-pal,

My name is Sheridan. I am from Mexico. I am sixteen years old. I am going to Ypsilanti Community High School, in tenth grade. My favorite job is playing soccer. My favorite soccer team is Manchester United, and Cruz Azul is a team for the Mexican people. I like to use my computer for forty minutes per day and play *FIFA 13*. I want to graduate and go to college and be able to help my mom in the future. I have one sister and one brother. I speak Spanish. What do you like to do?

From,

Sheridan Zaldivar

Dear Sheridan,

I am nine years old. I speak Thai and Laotian. I'm from Michigan but my family is from Thailand. My favorite sport is basketball. During Christmas, I have a Christmas party. What do you do for the holidays? My favorite food is Thai and Laos foods. What is your favorite food?

Sincerely,

Katie

....

Dear Katie,

My family does not celebrate Christmas because my dad goes to work. Then I have vacations. I like to use my computer and watch TV. My favorite food is everything Mexican. What do you like about Thailand?

From,

Sheridan

Dear Sheridan,

The things that I like about Thailand are the food and dresses. They get different colors and they have blessed bracelets. The people are very nice. Do you like visiting your aunt? They will not let you step on people's grass in Thailand because you can get hit, and it really hurts. I got two lucky bracelets and dresses. They can make papaya—they can make it spicy and not make it spicy. My favorite restaurant is Sala Thai. What about you? What is your favorite restaurant? What's your favorite hobby? I like to do back flips. What do you do every day?

Sincerely,

Katie

....

Dear Katie,

I don't like visiting my aunt. I don't have a favorite restaurant. My favorite hobby is playing soccer and *Grand Theft Auto*. I do this every day: go to school, go to my home, eat, use my computer and iPod, and last I go asleep. Do you like snow?

Sincerely,

Sheridan

Dear Sheridan,

I do like snow. I like snow because we can make snowmen and have snowball fights. Do you like snow? I really like *Grand Theft Auto,* too. I go to school every day and get on my tablet when I'm finished with my homework. My school is nice. My class has thirty-one people (as in students). I have some bullies in my class. What is your favorite TV show? Do you love your school? My school is like a family. What about your school? Is your school like a family, and what happens at your school? Is it wonderful at Ypsilanti Community High School? My school is like a family because I can learn more things in fourth grade. I'm in fourth grade. What grade are you in? What is it like every day at school? How is your school like a family?

Sincerely,

Katie J.

....

Dear Katie,

My school is not like a family because in high school the people are more bad; in my classes some people are nice. Only one class I like because every person is Latino. My favorite TV show is called *Familia Peluche*; it is a fun show. My school is fun because I change classes every forty-five minutes and I have gym every day. I am in tenth grade. What is your favorite show? What do you like about school? And I don't like snow because I work to clean snow with my dad. :-(

Sincerely,

Sheridan

Olaya Zapata

 Olaya Zapata is from the United States, but her parents are from Mexico and Texas. She is fifteen years old, born on January 3, 1999. She lives with her mom and stepdad, her sisters Elijah and Stephanie, and her brother Leroy. She enjoys spending time with her family more than with her friends. Her favorite color is red. She loves to take care of her siblings. She loves to clean and cook Hispanic food. She hopes to focus on her goals, which are to pass all her classes in order to graduate with the class of 2016.

AGE 16

Recipe for Enchiladas

This recipe for enchiladas is delicious. I learned how to make them by watching my mom cook in the kitchen. You can make any kind of rice you want and enjoy your enchiladas. I hope you like my recipe. I'm fifteen years old, and I love to cook Mexican food.

You can make as many as you want, but I usually make a cake pan full of them.

Estimated time: About thirty minutes to one hour

INGREDIENTS

- Tortillas (El Milagro), as many as you can eat
- Piece of garlic
- Oil
- *Chiles rojo* (red chiles), dried, Goya brand
- Cheese (any shredded cheese)
- Pot
- Strainer
- Stirring spoon
- Bowl
- Plate
- Fork
- Knife
- Coca-Cola
- Napkin to clean your mouth

DIRECTIONS

1. Get the red dried chiles and cut them open. Take out all the seeds. Then put a pot of water to boil, and put the dried red chiles in the pot and let them boil for ten minutes. Add a piece of garlic to the pot.

2. Then, get the blender and put the boiled red chiles in and blend it up. Get a bowl and a strainer and put the blended chiles in and stir so the seeds and skin don't come out.

3. Get a skillet and add a little bit of oil. Dip the tortilla in the enchilada sauce on both sides. Place it on the skillet, and add some shredded cheese. Then fold up the tortilla and let it cook for about a minute.

4. Take it out and serve it on your plate, and enjoy it with Coca-Cola!

First Day of School in the US

MY FIRST DAY OF SCHOOL was on a chilly afternoon in Toledo, Ohio, not knowing any English or anyone. I came from Pinos Zacatecas, Mexico—I was only three at the time. My parents came to the US with their family to find a job.

It was my first day of school in the US; I was seven at the time. The school was small, but now in 2014 it is big. I started to get nervous when I walked in the school. It looked different; the lockers were gray, and now they are yellow. I didn't understand anyone, and I felt like I didn't blend in with others. The teacher wouldn't tell the students anything when they would laugh at me. My teacher only spoke English and it was hard for me to understand anything she was telling me.

Then I felt like I was getting bullied because people would say stuff to me and laugh because I wouldn't know what they were saying. Some students would try to speak Spanish, but they couldn't and they would just laugh. I felt bullied in a class full of students who would make fun of others.

After being in class where I felt bullied, I met a girl named Stephanie. I met her later that day and she talked to me. She was short and had brown hair and tan skin. She wore jeans and a sweater. She came up and said, "Hi, are you new?" She was from a different part of Mexico. I felt a little shy when she came up to me. She spoke Spanish just like me but only a little bit of English. We started to talk and get to know each other well, and I met some of her Hispanic friends and we all hung out together. I met a lot of her friends who spoke Spanish. Then I felt welcomed at that school.

Then I was put in an English Language Arts class in high school with a lot of bilingual students and others who spoke Spanish. The classroom is big and has a lot of English words and meanings on the walls. I feel good because everyone treats one another like family. We share everything with each other. Now that I'm in this class, I know a lot of English, so it's easier to communicate with others.

My first day of school was important and memorable to me because it showed me that I wasn't the only one who felt shy and nervous on the first day of school. It's important to make friends so that you can talk to them and meet their friends.

Open Letter

Dear assistant principal,

To make our school a greater community, I have some ideas to improve it.

First, we need cleaner bathrooms. The seats are so dirty. The floor is full of trash and toilet paper. The floor is always wet. They should make more hall sweeps because too many people are late to class. (A hall sweep is when security guards clear the halls of students.)

I might be the best person to give this advice because I am a member of the community, and it's important for me.

My goal for coming from Mexico to the US is to learn and be a part of this school. My ELL class is the class where I feel more comfortable and happy, because I'm friends with everyone and we're like a family.

The things that this school does well is that they hired new security guards—and strong ones—to provide safety. I also like that there are no uniforms because everyone has the right to wear what they want. I hope YCHS will do everything that needs to be done.

Sincerely,

A student at YCHS

Janet Herrera

 Janet Herrera was born in Ypsilanti, Michigan. She speaks English and Spanish. She likes to play on the trampoline. She wants to be an author when she grows up.

AGE 7

Recipe for Yummy Tacos

INGREDIENTS

- Tortilla
- Chicken
- Cheese
- Tomatoes
- Lettuce

DIRECTIONS

1. First, you take out a tortilla.
2. Next, put chicken in the tortilla.
3. Then, put the cheese on top of the chicken.
4. Put the tomatoes on the cheese.
5. Last, put the lettuce on the tomatoes.
6. Eat it!

Pen-pal Letters

Dear pen-pal,

My name is Janet. I am seven years old. I go to Adams. My favorite subject is reading. My teacher's name is Ms. Todd. My favorite animal is a cat. What's your name? How old are you? What's your favorite animal? What language do you speak? I speak English and Spanish. What's your favorite candy?

Sincerely,

Janet

Dear pen-pal Janet,

My name is Olaya. I am fourteen years old. I go to Ypsilanti Community High School. I'm in ninth grade. It's my first year in high school. My favorite subject is English Language Arts. My teacher's name is Ms. Sirman. My favorite animal is a dog because they're cute to cuddle with. I speak Spanish and English. My family is from Pinos Zacatecas, Mexico. My favorite candy is *Paleta de Sandia*. Where are you from? What grade are you in? It's nice to meet you, Janet.

Sincerely,

Your pen-pal Olaya

P.S. *Paleta de Sandia* is a lollipop that looks like a watermelon but is a little spicy.

··

Dear pen-pal Olaya,

I like your letter. I was born in Michigan. My parents are from Mexico. I am in second grade. Do you have any friends? What is your job in high school? I know the *Paleta de Sandia*. I like it too. What is your favorite movie? I like Christmas. On Christmas, I open presents. For Christmas I am going to get a toy cat, number rug, tea set, and My Little Pony, and my cousins and my friends are going to give me presents. What is your favorite holiday?

Sincerely,

Your pen-pal Janet

Dear pen-pal Janet,

I like your letter. It's so adorable. I was born in Michigan too. What part are your parents from? I have a lot of friends. My job in high school is to get enough credits to graduate. My favorite movie is *El Chavo del Ocho*. I like Christmas too, because we make tamales and open gifts at 12AM on the 24th. What's your last name? My favorite holiday is Christmas.

Sincerely,

Your pen-pal Olaya

....

Dear pen-pal Olaya,

My family is from Mexico. Herrera is my last name. I make tamales on special days like Sunday. Saturday my dad makes them. Do you cook with your family? What do you do special? What did you do on New Year's? I have a Martin Luther King Jr. assembly. We all go together. It is cozy and warm. It's like a family. How is your school like a family? If I had a magic wand, all the books would be neat, the school would have decorations, at lunch we would eat spaghetti, hamburgers, and hot dogs, and all of the bullies would turn into nutcrackers.

What would you like to change about your school if you had a magic wand?

Sincerely,

Janet

Enjoy!

About 826michigan

826michigan is a nonprofit organization dedicated to supporting students ages 6 to 18 with their creative and expository writing skills, and to helping teachers inspire their students to write. Our services are structured around the understanding that great leaps in learning can happen with one-on-one attention, and that strong writing skills are fundamental to future success. With this in mind, we provide after-school tutoring, evening workshops, in-school residencies, help for English language learners, and provide publication opportunities for students. All of our programs are challenging and enjoyable, and ultimately strengthen each student's power to express ideas effectively, creatively, confidently, and in his or her individual voice.

TUTORING IS AT THE HEART OF IT

Our method is simple: we assign free tutors to students so that the students can get one-on-one help. It is our understanding that great advancement in English skills and homework comprehension can be made within hours if students are given concentrated help from knowledgeable tutor-mentors. We offer free tutoring four days a week at both of our writing labs, on Liberty Street in Ann Arbor and at beezy's cafe on Washington Street in Ypsilanti.

WORKSHOPS

We offer a number of free workshops taught by professional artists, writers, and our talented volunteers. From comic books to screenplays, bookmaking to radio, our wide variety of workshops are perfect for writers of all ages and interests.

IN-SCHOOL PROJECTS

Our trained volunteers go into local public schools every day to support teachers with their classroom writing assignments. Based on the teacher's curriculum, assignments range from writing tales to crafting five-paragraph essays.

FIELD TRIPS

We want to help teachers get their students excited about writing, while helping students be better able to express their ideas. We welcome teachers to bring their classes in for field trips during the school day. A group of volunteers, interns, and staff leads every field trip, whether we are solving mysteries, writing bedtime stories, or playing a life-sized poetry board game. Our most popular field trip is our Storytelling & Bookmaking workshop, which culminates in an orignial book for each student to take home.

OUR STORE

The Liberty Street Robot Supply & Repair, a one-stop shop for robots, robot owners, enthusiasts alike, is designed to inspire creativity and bring awareness to our programs to the community. Come visit us at 115 East Liberty Street in downtown Ann Arbor. All proceeds from our store directly fund our free programs. Onward robots!

—

115 East Liberty Street
Ann Arbor, MI 48104
734.761.3463
826michigan.org

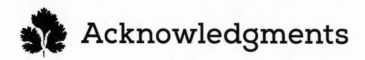

Acknowledgments

Our tremendous gratitude to the following people cannot be overstated. It takes a village to bring a publication into being and each of these individuals has been instrumental in this process.

Ypsilanti Community Schools

Unending thanks to the following teachers and administrators for opening up their classrooms and schools, collaborating on all of the curriculum, and serving as incredible educators and role models for their students.

Liz Sirman
YCHS ELL Teacher

Shannon Fitzgerald
Adams STEM Academy ELL Teacher

Abukar Abas
Paraprofessional Teacher & Translator

Scott Menzel
YCS Superintendent

Justin Jennings
YCHS Principal

Connie Thompson
Adams STEM Academy Principal

826michigan

Our heartfelt appreciation to our heroic volunteers who generously offered their time and talents every step along the way. They made it possible for our students to have individualized one-on-one attention and writing support and worked behind-the-scenes on each element of the publication process.

Lauren Koski
On-site Project Coordinator

In-school Residency Volunteers

Bryan Frederick, Kristin Jordan, Nancy Koziol, Ariana Orozco, Terra Reed

Traveling Editors

Seyram Avle, Aneesha Badrinarayan, Robyn Charles, Zia Davidian, Jill Epstein, Pat Gold, Barbara MacKenzie, Elizabeth Mitchell, Drew Phillips, Alyssa Selasky, Jim Wright

Copyeditors
Nicole Brugger-Dethmers, Jessi
Carrothers, Jill Epstein, Megan Gilson,
Kimberly Huebner, Rachael Jackson, Erica
Jolokai, Jennifer Pulling, Rachel Rickard,
Alex Schillinger, Kati Shanks, Roger Valade

Typists and Organizational
Assistants
Kimberly Huebner, Dane Larsen,
Barbara MacKenzie, Kati Shanks

Curriculum Development
Sarah Campbell, Gabe Carlson,
Lauren Koski, Kailee Sosnowski

Designers
Kevin Woodland
Lead Designer

Jill Epstein
Design Assistant

Community Supporters
Immense gratitude to our sponsors and
supporters, who have truly made this a
community-wide collaboration.

Thomson-Shore

Zingerman's Community of Businesses

Many thanks to our esteemed friends in
the local food community for contributing
recipes.

CONVERSIONS

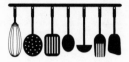

1 DEGREE CELSIUS	=	1.8 DEGREES FAHRENHEIT
1 TABLESPOON	=	3 TEASPOONS
1 CUP	=	8 FLUID OUNCES
1 GALLON	=	8 PINTS
1 PINT	=	16 FLUID OUNCES
1 GALLON	=	3.8 LITERS
1 KILOGRAM	=	2.2 POUNDS
1 OUNCE	=	28 GRAMS
1 TEASPOON	=	60 DROPS
1 CUP	=	2 GILLS
1 PECK	=	2 GALLONS
1 BUSHEL	=	4 PECKS
1 PENNYWEIGHT	=	1/20 OUNCE
1 PINCH	=	1 DASH
1 DASH	=	LESS THAN ⅛ TEASPOON
1 POTTLE	=	2 QUARTS
1 CUP FLOUR	=	ABOUT 150 GRAMS FLOUR
1 CUP WATER	=	ABOUT 237 GRAMS WATER

TRANSLATIONS

SPANISH	•	BUEN PROVECHO
ARABIC	•	ISTALAZZA
SOMALI	•	HA KUU MACAANAATO
SWAHILI	•	FURAHIENI CHAKULA CHENU
FRENCH	•	BON APPÉTIT
PORTUGUESE	•	BOM APETITE
LAOTIAN	•	MI KHUAAM SUK DAN A HAN KHONG THAN
VIETNAMESE	•	ĂN NGON NHÉ
AMHARIC	•	MELKAM MEGEB
THAI	•	ขอให้เจริญอาหาร
ENGLISH	•	ENJOY YOUR MEAL
CHINESE	•	請慢用
HAWAI'IAN	•	E 'AI KĀKOU
HINDI	•	कृपया भोजन का आनंद लीजिये
ICELANDIC	•	VERÐI ÞÉR AÐ GÓÐU
RUSSIAN	•	ПРИЯТНОГО АППЕТИТА
SWEDISH	•	SMAKLIG MÅLTID!
TAGALOG	•	KAINAN NA!
WELSH	•	MWYNHEWCH EICH BWYD
XHOSA	•	UKONWABELE UKUTYA KWAKHO